THE COZY CHICKS KITCHEN is chock full of mouthwatering gems. Everything is here: main dishes, desserts, salads, soups, drinks, and did I mention desserts? Don't miss this fabulous collection. I've got both the ebook version and a hardcopy. Get yours today!

— *Julie Hyzy*, *New York Times* bestselling author of the White House Chef and Manor House mysteries

The Cozy Chicks Kitchen

The Cozy Chicks, LLC

DEDICATION

To our readers.

You buy our books,
you write to us,
you read our blog,
you comment on Facebook,
you support us in every way.
In other words, you have become our friends.
Thank you!

WELCOME TO OUR KITCHEN!

Pull up a stool and let us pour you a cup of coffee. We'll have a chat as a pot of tomato basil soup bubbles on the stove. While the soup is simmering, feel free to sit back, relax, and listen to the sizzle of lemon chicken cutlets crisping to a golden brown in the frying pan. By the time we catch up on work and family and start discussing the last book we've read, the buttery, cinnamon scents of the apple ginger pie baking in the oven will curl around our shoulders like a warm shawl and coax a sigh of contentment from our lips.

Friends, food, and fellowship. That is what home feels like. And the kitchen is the heart of the home. This sense of warmth and companionship is what The Cozy Chicks try to invoke in our novels. And now, our cookbook will allow you to enter the heart of our cozy mystery worlds—the stories of our characters and of their authors, told through food. For a short while, our protagonists have taken a break from crime solving to don aprons and wield spatulas and wooden spoons. And they'd like nothing more than to spend some time with you.

Enjoy!

The Cozy Chicks

We are:
Ellery Adams / J.B. Stanley
Deb Baker / Hannah Reed
Lorraine Bartlett / L.L. Bartlett / Lorna Barrett
Kate Collins
Mary Kennedy
Mary Jane Maffini
Maggie Sefton
Leann Sweeney

www.CozyChicksBlog.com

STARTERS

PIZZA DIP

by Lorraine Bartlett / LL Bartlett

Katie Bonner, of the **Victoria Square Mysteries,** dates the owner of the Square's pizza parlor. While she loves pizza, she doesn't want to eat an entire pie in one sitting. Instead, she often makes this dip. So it isn't really a pizza—it's got a lot of the same flavors and is great when she wants the taste, but not the calories of a whole pizza.

INGREDIENTS
1 package (8 ounces) cream cheese, softened
3 teaspoons Italian seasoning
¼ teaspoon garlic powder
2 cups (8 ounces) shredded mozzarella cheese
1 cup Parmesan cheese
½ cup pizza sauce
½ cup finely chopped green pepper
½ cup finely chopped sweet red pepper

Preheat the oven to 350°. In a bowl, combine the cream cheese, Italian seasoning, and garlic powder. Spread on the bottom of a greased 9-inch pie plate. Combine the cheeses and sprinkle half the mix over the cream cheese layer. Top with the pizza sauce and peppers. Sprinkle with the remaining cheeses. Bake for 20 minutes. Serve warm with crackers, chips, or pretzels.

Yield: 3½ cups.

MYSTERIOUS BRIE

by Mary Jane Maffini

Those of us who read and write mysteries love surprises. We like things that turn out unexpectedly. This appetizer is a blend of interesting ingredients and the whole is much more than the sum of the parts. And so the plot thickens.

INGREDIENTS
1 pound wheel of Brie
½ cup sun-dried tomatoes, chopped coarsely and
    soaked in hot water for 30 minutes, then drained
1 tablespoon lemon juice
1–2 tablespoons olive oil
¼ cup pesto (store-bought is fine
freshly ground pepper.

Preheat the oven to 350°. Slice the Brie in half horizontally. Place the bottom layer in a pretty baking dish that you can also serve from. Process the sun-dried tomatoes in a food processor until chopped fine. Add the lemon and oil and purée. Spread the bottom layer of Brie with the pesto. Don't go quite to the edge. Spread the sun-dried tomatoes over that. Again, don't go quite to the edge. Add the fresh pepper. Cover with the second Brie layer and press a bit to bond them. Bake for about 10 minutes. You want the ingredients to just soften, not to melt. Serve with slices of crusty bread, crackers, or raw veggies.

Yield: 6-8 servings

KATE'S HUMMUS

by Kate Collins

I love hummus on pita chips and am always tinkering with recipes to make my own. Here's a great starter recipe. You can add your choice of flavors. Mine is minced red or yellow sweet peppers and finely chopped Kalamata olives.

INGREDIENTS
1 14-ounce can chickpeas, drained
4 tablespoons Tahini sauce
¼ cup lemon juice
1 clove garlic, peeled
1-2 teaspoon sea salt to taste (optional)
⅓ cup water
paprika

Blend the first 4 ingredients in a food processor, adding water gradually to keep the machine running. The consistency should be smooth and creamy. Empty the contents into a bowl. Sprinkle with paprika. This will keep for weeks but should be refrigerated.

Yield: 2 cups

CREAMY CHIPPED BEEF DIP

by Maggie Sefton

I've served this appetizer dip for years and years. I tinkered around with several recipes until I found this combination of flavors. It's always a crowd-pleaser and works for any occasion. It can be served with crackers or all sorts of veggies. It's perfect for potlucks and picnics, football parties, holiday open houses, or any social get-together.

INGREDIENTS
16 ounce cream cheese, softened
4 tablespoons cream or milk
1 cup sour cream
2 2½-ounce packages dried deli beef, diced
½ cup finely grated onion
½ teaspoon black pepper
4 tablespoons butter
¼ cup or more bottled Worcestershire sauce, to taste

Preheat the oven to 350°. Cream and the beat softened cream cheese with the milk or cream. Add sour cream, dried beef, onion, and pepper. Mix well, then add Worcestershire sauce to taste. Stir until blended, then put in a casserole dish. Bake for 20 minutes. Let cool slightly. Best served warm, not hot. Serve with crackers or veggies.

Yield: 3 cups

SALSA TO DIE FOR

by Hannah Reed (aka Deb Baker)

Story Fischer, of the **Queen Bee Mysteries,** grows tomatillos in her backyard garden every year. They sprout like weeds and taste magnificent in this easy salsa. Not only that, they bloom profusely, which keeps Story's honeybees happy gathering nectar. (This recipe also appears in **Buzz Off,** from the first **Queen Bee Mystery.**)

INGREDIENTS
20 tomatillos
1 onion, quartered
2 jalapenos (or to taste)
4 Anaheim peppers
cilantro (optional)
salt to taste

Preheat the oven to 425°. Roast the tomatillos, onion, and peppers for 15 minutes. Put the roasted vegetables in a food processor with the cilantro and pulse until coarsely chopped. Add salt.

Yield: 6 servings

ONION BREADSTICKS

by Lorraine Bartlett / LL Bartlett

Onions are good for you. They're an antioxidant. They help to neutralize free radicals in your body. Onions are thought to prevent heart disease. Okay, you may shed a few tears when you peel and cut them, but it's worth the pain (and squinting). And these easy-to-make breadsticks are worth the time to prepare them. (It's just the dough rising that takes time—otherwise they're easy and fun.)

INGREDIENTS
1 large sweet onion, halved and
    thinly sliced
6 tablespoons butter, divided
1 teaspoon sugar
1 loaf (1 pound) frozen bread dough, thawed

In a large skillet, over medium heat, cook the onion in 4 tablespoons of butter for 5 minutes or until tender. Add the sugar; cook over low heat for 30-40 minutes more, or until the onion is golden brown, stirring frequently.

On a lightly floured surface, roll the bread dough into an 18-inch x 12-inch rectangle. Spoon the onion mixture lengthwise over half the dough. Fold the plain half of the dough over the onion mixture. Cut into 18 1-inch strips. Twist each strip twice; pinch the ends to seal.

Place each piece of twisted dough 2 inches apart on a prepared baking sheet. Melt the remaining butter and brush it over the breadsticks. Cover and let rise in a warm place until the dough has doubled in size (about 40-45 minutes).

Preheat the oven to 350°. Bake for 12 to 15 minutes or until lightly browned. Serve warm.

Yield: 18 pieces.

ARTICHOKE DIP

by Mary Kennedy

Sometimes Ali and Taylor Blake like to serve crackers and hot artichoke dip in **The Dream Club Mysteries.** This is so simple and you probably have the ingredients on hand.

INGREDIENTS
1 14-ounce) jar of artichokes, drained and chopped
1 cup mayonnaise
1 cup grated Parmesan cheese

Preheat the oven to 375°. Mix all the ingredients together and place in a greased 9 x 13-inch baking dish. Bake 15-20 minutes, or until bubbly and golden brown. Serve with crackers, bagel chips, or toast points.

Yield: 6-8 servings

SOUTH OF THE BORDER SHRIMP COCKTAIL
by Deb Baker (aka Hannah Reed)

I first discovered this appetizer while sitting in Rocky Point, Mexico, on a colorful deck watching life go by. Pelicans, piñatas, and Mexican salsa music; a perfect afternoon. As soon as I returned home, I started experimenting and kept at it until I got it right. Serve to your guests in martini or big rimmed wine glasses.

INGREDIENTS
1 small bottle (6 ounces) clam juice
1 small can (5.5 ounces) Spicy V8 vegetable juice
1 (4-5 ounces) can of bay shrimp, diced
1 stalk of celery, diced
4-5 green onions, diced
juice from ½ lime
a handful of cilantro (optional)

In a medium-sized bowl, mix together the above ingredients. Chill and serve.

Yield: 4 servings

MEDITERRANIAN-STYLE CROSTINI APPETIZERS
by Kate Collins

Here's a real crowd-pleasing appetizer that's easy to make and delicious even reheated the next day.

INGREDIENTS
1 long, skinny baguette, approximately 12 inches
1 clove garlic, minced
¼ cup extra virgin olive oil
creamy goat cheese (5-6 ounces) room temperature
Olive tapanade (approximately 4-ounces Kalamata or
    Greek flavored, if possible)
Fresh tomato-onion salsa, or 1 large diced tomato and
    1 small diced onion

Preheat the oven to 375°. In a saucepan, simmer the garlic in the olive oil until the oil is well flavored. Cut the bread into ½ inch thick rounds and brush each piece with garlic oil. Spread the tapanade on slices as thick as desired, sprinkle salsa over it, then top each slice with a dollop of goat cheese. Arrange on a baking sheet. Bake until golden. Serve and enjoy. (This recipe can be prepared ahead of time and baked just before your guests arrive.)

Yield: approximately 24 pieces

FOOTBALL TOUCHDOWN SPREAD
by Deb Baker (aka Hannah Reed)

Here in Wisconsin, we take our Packers seriously. Up in the Michigan Upper Peninsula, Gertie Johnson, of the ***Backwoods-Yooper Mysteries,*** roots for the Packers, too. The U.P., as the locals call it, should have been part of Wisconsin, because when Detroit plays Green Bay, the Yoopers wear their green and gold. During football season, I like to experiment with half-time appetizers. Here's one of my favorites.

INGREDIENTS
1 pound white cheddar cheese, shredded
1 medium red onion, grated and juices wrung out
2 tablespoons mayonnaise
raspberry preserves
salty crackers

Blend the first 3 ingredients and spread on a platter (about ¼ inch thick). Top with a generous layer of the raspberry preserves. Serve with crackers

Yield: 6 servings

SATISFYING SOUPS

SPEEDY GUACAMOLE SOUP
by Mary Jane Maffini

None of my main characters can cook. Sure, they can buy take-out and get invited to dinner, but that's about it. I worry about their ability to survive their adventurous lives so I'm offering easy recipes to them. Here's my favorite suggestion for Charlotte Adams, the professional organizer and amateur sleuth, who starts her adventures in *Organize Your Corpses.* As a rule there's nothing but Ben & Jerry's New York Super Fudge Chunk in her freezer. Still, even Charlotte could make either variation of this soup. It's delicious. It contains vegetables and it's almost as easy as eating ice cream.

INGREDIENTS
2 cups chicken broth (homemade or low-sodium canned or boxed)
1 ripe avocado, peeled and diced
sour cream
salsa

Bring the broth to a boil. Add the avocado and whip with a stick blender until smooth. Or transfer to a blender or food processor and process until creamy. Ladle into bowls and top with a dollop of sour cream and you're ready to go. This is yummy enough for a dinner party, not that Charlotte would ever have one.

Yield: 2 servings

STUFFED PEPPER SOUP

by Lorraine Bartlett / LL Bartlett

I'm a sucker for stuffed peppers, and I'm always looking for a new way to make them. Okay, so this isn't
exactly a stuffed pepper—but it tastes like it. And it's
wonderful on a cool fall evening, along with some
nice crusty bread (and a thick layer of butter).

INGREDIENTS
2 pounds ground sausage (mild or spicy, your
    choice)
2 quarts water
1 28-ounces can diced tomatoes, do not drain
1 28-ounces can tomato sauce
2 cups cooked long grain white rice
2 cups chopped green pepper
¼ cup brown sugar, firmly packed
1 teaspoon salt
1 teaspoon ground black pepper

In a large saucepan or Dutch oven, brown the sausage
and drain. Add the remaining ingredients and bring
to a boil. Reduce the heat. Cover and simmer for 30-
40 minutes or until the peppers are tender. Serve with
a loaf of warm, crusty bread.

Yield: 8-10 servings

SOUTHERN OKRA SOUP
by Deb Baker (aka Hannah Reed)

My dad was born and raised in Arkansas, so even though I grew up in the Midwest, we ate corn bread, grits, black-eyed peas, and of course, okra. It isn't usually available fresh here in Wisconsin, and doesn't grow well in our short summers, but the frozen variety works well in this soup.

INGREDIENTS
1 medium onion, chopped
1 cup red bell pepper, chopped
3 cloves of garlic, minced
2 bay leaves
1 teaspoon thyme
2 teaspoons paprika
2 teaspoons Old Bay seasoning
½ teaspoon pepper, or to taste
¼ teaspoon red pepper flakes, or to taste
2 14.5-ounces cans diced tomatoes with green
    chilies (I like Red Gold Petite)
2 cans water (use the tomato cans)
1 pound okra, frozen
1 15-ounce can garbanzo beans
1 15-ounce can kidney beans

Cook the onion until soft; about 5 minutes. Add the red pepper and garlic and cook 1 or 2 minutes. Add all the spices and cook 1 minute. Add everything else and cook until the okra is done and all the ingredients have melded.

Yield: 8-10 servings

CREAMY TOMATO SOUP

by Mary Kennedy

Everyone at WYME Radio in the **Talk Radio Mysteries** has to eat on the run, and Vera Mae Atkins loves to bring in homemade soup for the crowd. This is one of her favorites.

INGREDIENTS
1 onion, diced
4 tablespoons butter
2 cans (14-ounces) diced tomatoes
1 46-ounce can tomato juice
1 tablespoon chicken bouillon paste
3 tablespoons sugar
12 ounces heavy cream (you can use fat-free half and
    half)
1 cup cooking sherry
fresh basil or parsley

Sauté the diced onion in butter. Add the canned tomatoes, tomato juice, bouillon paste, and sugar. Heat almost to the boiling point and then remove from the heat. Add the cream and sherry and sprinkle the parsley or basil on the top.

Yield: 6 servings

STORY'S SUMMERTIME BEET SOUP

by Hannah Reed (aka Deb Baker)

Story Fischer's garden has always been bountiful, mainly because of her honeybees. Those little girls spread joy wherever they go. The Thai chili pepper gives this recipe a little heat, but not too much. Serve chilled on a hot summer day or warm when it rains. (This recipe also appears in *Buzz Off,* from the first **Queen Bee Mystery.**)

INGREDIENTS
1 pound beets, peeled and diced
1 medium onion, diced
1 large carrot, diced
1 clove garlic, minced
3 tablespoons ginger, minced
1 Thai chili pepper (optional)
2 tablespoons sugar
2 cups water
2 cups chicken broth
½ teaspoon salt
½ teaspoon white pepper
whipping cream
chives

Put all the ingredients except salt, pepper, cream, and chives into a pot and bring to a boil. Reduce the heat and simmer for 15 minutes or until tender. Add the salt and pepper. Cool slightly. Strain and reserve the liquid from the pot. Puree the cooked vegetables in the food processor. Combine the liquid and vegetables, stir in a little whipping cream to taste. Serve warm or chilled. Garnish bowls with chopped chives.

Yield: 6 servings

IRISH LEEK AND POTATO SOUP
by Kate Collins

Everyone loves a good Irish recipe for St. Patrick's Day, but this is one I found works well all year round. It's become a family favorite. If you want to make a meal of it, toss ham chunks in for the last 10 minutes, serve with crusty bread and enjoy. As the Irish say, Sláinte!

INGREDIENTS
¼ cup olive oil
1 cup onion, ¼ inch dice
2 diced leeks, well rinsed
2 tablespoons all-purpose flour
5 cups chicken stock
4 cups diced Idaho potatoes or 1 5-pound bag new
    red potatoes
1 large carrot, diced
salt and pepper to taste
chives (optional)
bacon bits (optional)
bouquet garni (see page 17)

Melt the butter in a saucepan over medium high heat. Lower the heat; add the onion and carrots and cook gently for 2 minutes. Add the leeks and cook for 6-7 minutes or until the onions are soft but not brown. Add the flour and stir for 2 minutes to thicken, making a roux, without browning. Add the chicken stock and bring to a boil. Add the bouquet garni. Add the potatoes and simmer over medium heat for 40-45 minutes or until the potatoes are cooked thoroughly. Remove from the heat and discard the garni. Garnish with bacon bits or chives.

Yield: 4 servings

BOUQUET GARNI:
1 bay leaf,
2 tablespoons chopped parsley
¼ teaspoon dried thyme,
¼ teaspoon black peppercorns.

Tie the ingredients in a small piece of cheesecloth or wrap in foil pricked with small holes.

TOMATO SOUP WITH THAI BASIL

by Deb Baker (aka Hannah Reed)

Story Fischer, of the **Queen Bee Mysteries,** loves growing tomatoes—all different kinds. She especially likes Amish paste tomatoes and Beefsteaks. In September when she has an abundance of juicy, ripe tomatoes, she makes this soup, using Thai basil, which gives it an exotic flavor. She freezes some for those snowy Wisconsin winter days.

INGREDIENTS
3 cups onions, chopped
6 cloves of garlic, minced
12 cups of tomatoes, coarsely chopped
2 cups water
2 teaspoons of sugar or substitute
2 tablespoons kosher salt
1 small container (½ pint) heavy cream
green onions, chopped (for optional garnish)
Thai basil (for optional garnish)

Cook the onions until soft. Add the garlic and cook a few more minutes. Add the tomatoes, water, salt, and sugar. Simmer for one hour or until the tomatoes start breaking down. Puree, strain to remove the tomato skins. Serve with a dollop of cream. Garnish with green onions and Thai basil.

Yield: 8 servings

EAST COAST CHOWDER
by Mary Jane Maffini

The characters in the **Camilla MacPhee Mysteries** originally hail from the east coast of Canada where chowder is wonderful and, if you visit, you're likely to be offered a bowl. Lucky for Camilla (an entirely undomesticated lawyer), she has three bossy sisters living near her in Ottawa. They are excellent cooks, if a bit inclined to offer unsolicited advice with dinner. Still, it's worth being bossed around a bit to score a bowl of this chowder on a wintery night.

INGREDIENTS
1 pound haddock filet
½ pound salmon fillet
½ large onion sliced
1 large bay leaf
3-4 potatoes cubed (or whatever shape you like!)
1 large carrot, chopped
6 slices of bacon (chopped)
½ large onion, chopped fine
1 stalk of celery, chopped fine
2 tablespoons butter
2 tablespoons all-purpose flour
1 cup milk
1 cup cream
1/3 pound sea scallops (cut up if large)
a tablespoon or two of lemon juice
a dash of Worcestershire sauce
salt and pepper to taste

Cover the haddock and salmon with water, add the onion and bay leaf, plus a bit of salt. Bring to a boil and simmer about twenty minutes. Drain, reserving the liquid, and remove the onion and bay leaf. Meanwhile, boil the potatoes, carrots, and a bit of salt together until cooked but not mushy. Sauté the bacon, add the chopped onion and celery, and cook until onion is nicely caramelized. Drain the cooked potatoes and carrots and add to the bacon-and-onion mixture. Melt the butter, add the flour and cook for 2 minutes. Do not let it brown. Add the milk, cream, and scallops, and bring to a boil. Cook for 2 minutes until the scallops are done. Add the cream mixture to the potatoes, bacon, etc. Add the drained fish, breaking into reasonable sized pieces. If the chowder is too thick, thin it with a bit of reserved fish stock. Add the lemon juice (or more if you like) and a splash of Worcestershire. Simmer for 5-10 minutes. You can make this a day ahead and reheat it.

Yield: 2 full servings or 4 small servings

SALADS & VEGGIES

JILLIAN'S FAVORITE SPINACH SALAD
by Leann Sweeney

The **Cats in Trouble Mysteries** feature quilter Jillian Hart and her three beloved cats, who join forces to help solve crimes in the small town of Mercy, South Carolina. Jillian is always busy quilting, volunteering at the local no-kill animal shelter or helping her best friend, Deputy Candace Carson, solve a mystery or two. She limits her time in the kitchen and likes quick and easy meals. Since she's a salad lover, this lovely spinach salad is perfect for hot Southern summers.

This recipe is big enough to share with her friend Candace, her love interest, Tom Stewart, and her step-daughter, Kara. This salad sparkles if served in a big glass punch bowl. But never ask her cats—Merlot, Chablis and Syrah—if they enjoy salad. Unless you're talking about tuna fish salad, of course.

INGREDIENTS
1 large bag or plastic box of fresh spinach (about 2 pounds)
2 pints of ripe, fresh strawberries, sliced
2 ounces of sliced almonds and 2 ounces of slivered almonds toasted
OR a small bag of sweetened, roasted walnuts
1 bottle of Brianna's Blush Wine Vinaigrette
OR make your own dressing:
⅓ cup granulated sugar
¼ cup apple cider vinegar
1½ teaspoon finely chopped onion
¼ teaspoon paprika
¼ teaspoon Worcestershire sauce

¼ cup vegetable oil
1 tablespoon poppy seeds (optional)

Combine the first 5 dressing ingredients in a blender and blend on high for 30 seconds. Slowly add the oil and poppy seeds. Mix the spinach, almonds, and strawberries in a large bowl. Add the dressing and toss right before serving.

Yield: 6 servings

ELLERY'S WARM CHICKEN SALAD

by Ellery Adams

Laurel Hobbs, the over-scheduled working mom in the **Books By the Bay Mysteries,** doesn't have much time to spend in the kitchen. She tries to fix quick, easy meals that are good for her family and this is one of their favorites. Serve on toast, a nice croissant, or on a bed of fresh greens.

INGREDIENTS
3 cups cooked chicken, cubed
1 cup green seedless grapes, halved
1 cup sliced celery (optional)
1 cup mayonnaise
½ cup toasted slivered almonds
2 tablespoons lemon juice
2 tablespoons onion, finely chopped
½ teaspoon salt
½ cup grated Parmesan cheese
½ cup breadcrumbs

Preheat the oven to 325°. Lightly grease a 2-quart baking dish. In a large bowl, mix all the ingredients except for the grated cheese and the breadcrumbs. Spoon the mixture into the baking dish. Mix the cheese and bread crumbs together and sprinkle them over the chicken mixture. Bake in the preheated oven until warm and the cheese is melted, approximately 20 minutes.

Yield: 4 servings

BROCCOLI APPLE SALAD

by Lorraine Bartlett / LL Bartlett

New York State, home of the ***Victoria Square Mysteries,*** is #2 when it comes to US apple production, and there are lots of great apple recipes to go with the wonderful apples grown there. This one is really good for you. Fruit, veggies, nuts, and dairy. (And it covers just about every food group, too.) And simple to make? Just try it. It goes great as a dish-to-pass at potluck dinners, as well.

INGREDIENTS
6 cups fresh broccoli florets
1½ cups cubed cheddar cheese
1 large red apple, cubed
1 cup coarsely chopped pecans
1 small red onion, chopped
½ cup red wine vinaigrette (or your favorite
    vinaigrette dressing)
½ teaspoon lemon juice

Combine the first five ingredients in a large salad bowl. Combine the vinaigrette and lemon juice; drizzle over the salad. Toss to coat.

Yield: 8-10 servings

PRETTY PANTRY FRUIT SALAD

by Leann Sweeney

Karen Stewart, mother to Jillian Hart's love interest, Tom, in the ***Cats in Trouble Mysteries***, says this winter fruit salad is so pretty that it should always be served in a glass bowl to show it off. Karen uses a trifle bowl and sets this salad in the center of the table when she has Tom and Jillian over for supper. Since Karen is one of the best cooks Jillian has ever known, she asked for this recipe and was surprised how simple it was to put together.

INGREDIENTS
1 21-ounce can Comstock peach pie filling (store brand not recommended)
1 15-ounce can mandarin orange slices, drained
1 20-ounce can chunk pineapple in its own juice, drained
1 12-ounce bag or 1 box of frozen strawberries, thawed
2-3 bananas, sliced

Combine all the fruit but the bananas in a large bowl. Refrigerate. Just before serving, add the sliced bananas. Put into a pretty glass bowl and serve.

Yield: 6 servings

FRENCH LENTIL SALAD

by Mary Jane Maffini/Victoria Abbott

This is a great dish to take to a pot-luck party. Put on some music while you do that chopping. You can mix and match ingredients. It's never the same twice, but it's always a hit. It's great as a leftover, too. You can serve the feta cheese separately if dairy is an issue. You may want to add a bit more salt in that case.

DRESSING
¼ cup extra virgin olive oil
3 tablespoon red wine vinegar
1 clove garlic, finely chopped
2 teaspoon Dijon mustard
1-2 teaspoons maple syrup
1 tablespoon chopped parsley
juice of half a lemon

VEGETABLES FOR SALAD
1 can of lentils, rinsed and drained, or two cups of
    cooked drained lentils (give or take).
½ red pepper chopped
3-4 green onions thinly sliced, white and green parts
1 yellow tomato, seeded and chopped
Or ½ yellow pepper and 1 red tomato, seeded and
    chopped
Or shredded carrots–whichever you prefer–I prefer
    what I have on hand
½ cup of celery chopped
6 ounces feta cheese, cubed or crumbled (optional)
1 teaspoon sea salt
½ teaspoon freshly ground pepper just before serving

In a small bowl or pitcher, combine the dressing ingredients with a wire whisk until smooth and creamy. Add the chopped veggies to a good-sized salad bowl, mixing them well. Add dressing and stir to cover veggies. Add feta if using. The longer you leave the dressing, the better it gets. By the way, this is our go-to dressing for bean salads too.

Yield: 6 servings

EASY CRISPY POTATOES

by Kate Collins

Serve these just once and you'll become a lifetime fan. Try it on your family and watch their faces when they taste them. Yummmm!

INGREDIENTS
2¾ cup chicken broth, sodium free
2 tablespoons unsalted butter
4 small unpeeled potatoes (Yukon gold are the best) washed
sea salt and pepper to taste

In a medium saucepan or small skillet, pour the broth over the potatoes so that they are half covered. Drop in the butter in pats. Cover and cook over medium heat for 20 minutes, or until the potatoes are fork tender. Remove the lid and let the liquid evaporate. Use the bottom of a glass to press down on the potato until it splits a little. Put sea salt and pepper on top of each potato. Turn over and let brown on the bottom. Salt and pepper the top. Turn to let the top brown. Voila! Delicious, crispy potatoes.

Yield: 4 servings

CHEESY CHIVE POTATOES
by Lorraine Bartlett/ LL Bartlett

Artisans Alley, in the **Victoria Square Mysteries,** is known for its fine arts and crafts. (And, unfortunately, some not-so-fine arts and crafts, too.) The vendors at Artisans Alley are known for their famous potluck dinners. With more than 60 artists, that's a lot of dishes to pass. Rose Nash is famous for the various potato dishes she prepares and this one never fails to please.

INGREDIENTS
6 medium potatoes, peeled and cubed
½ cup milk
½ cup shredded cheddar cheese
¼ teaspoon salt
⅛ teaspoon pepper
2 tablespoons minced fresh chives

Place the potatoes into a large saucepan and cover with water. Bring to a boil. Reduce the heat; cover and boil for 10-15 minutes or until tender. Drain the potatoes and add the milk, cheese, butter, salt, and pepper; mash. Stir in the chives.

Yield: 6 servings

CORN CASSEROLE

by Mary Jane Maffini

We all find times when we need to whip up a tasty side dish but we're too busy to shop. Maybe a book deadline (ahem). Enter corn casserole to the rescue. Chances are good you'll have the ingredients in your fridge and cupboard.

INGREDIENTS

2 tablespoons butter

2 tablespoons all-purpose flour

1 12-ounce can of corn niblets, drained, with liquid saved. (Of course, in the summer when corn is fresh, you could make a snazzy dish with delicious fresh corn.)

milk added to corn liquid to make 1 cup

2 large eggs, room temperature, lightly beaten

salt and pepper to taste

paprika (optional)

Optional: 2 tablespoons chopped parsley and chopped green onion sautéed in butter

Optional: ½ chopped red pepper, chopped ham or cooked crumbled bacon.

Optional: 2 tablespoons chopped mild (or hot!) green chilies.

Preheat the oven to 375°. Melt the butter and add the flour. Stir for two minutes over medium heat. It will foam up nicely. Try not to let it brown (although the world won't end if it does). Add the milk (and corn liquid) and bring to a boil, stirring until it thickens. Add the corn and seasonings. Add the beaten eggs and any of the optional suggestions (red pepper and ham are particularly fabulous!) or anything else you decide to toss in. Transfer to a buttered baking dish and bake for 30 minutes (or until the top is set). There you have it, easy, tasty and the price is right.

Yield: 4 servings

BAKED CRISPY POTATOES

by Kate Collins

This is our go-to potato dish. It's the healthy version of potato chips and will go with sandwiches as well as a meat entrée. For variety, throw on other cheese toppings just before the potatoes come out of the oven.

INGREDIENTS
3 medium-large potatoes, sliced very thin
½ cup Parmesan cheese
seasoned salt or smoky black sea salt

Set oven to 450°. Spray a baking sheet with oil spray. Lay potato slices end to end on the sheet. Sprinkle with a little seasoned salt, and parmesan cheese as thick as desired. Bake until browned and puffy, about 10 to 15 minutes.

Serves 3-4 servings

GRILLED CORN WITH ANCHO HONEY BUTTER
by Hannah Reed (aka Deb Baker)

You know you are deep into summer when the farmers' markets and roadside stands offer ripe corn on the cob. Drive along the rustic road and stop in Moraine, Wisconsin. You'll find the cutest little stand right in the heart of the community. Here's Story Fischer's favorite way to serve it. (This recipe also appears in **Plan Bee**, from the third **Queen Bee Mystery.**)

INGREDIENTS
6 ears corn on the cob
1 ancho chili, minced if fresh. If dry, tear in pieces,
    soak in warm water 30 minutes and drain
1 stick (½ cup) unsalted butter, softened
3 cloves of garlic
¼ cup cilantro
1 tablespoon lime juice
1 tablespoon honey
1½ teaspoons kosher salt
pepper to taste

In a food processor, chop the cilantro and garlic. Add the chili, lime juice, honey, salt, and pepper. Add the butter and blend until smooth. Toss the unshucked ears on the grill and cook over high heat until the husks are charred, about 10 to 15 minutes. Serve with ancho honey butter.

Or shuck the ears, brush with ancho honey butter and grill for about 10 minutes.

Yield: 6 servings

MARINATED CARROTS
by Leann Sweeney

Jillian Hart, cat lover, quilter and chief mystery solver in the **Cats in Trouble Mysteries**, was raised by her grandparents in Texas and this easy family recipe came with her when Jillian moved to Mercy, South Carolina with her wonderful cats—all Hurricane Katrina rescues. Her grandmother's recipes were all just "do this" and "add that," so if this recipe seems unusual in its lack of specifics, that's just how Jillian's grandma worked. Since Jillian watched her grandma make it many times, she doesn't need too many directions either.

INGREDIENTS
Carrots
1 sweet onion, sliced thin
1-2 celery stalks, chopped
1 15-ounce can chickpeas (garbanzo beans)
1 11-ounce bottle Italian dressing or vinaigrette
    (balsamic works well)

Cook as many carrots as you like until tender, but not soggy. Cool and slice. Place in an appropriate size bowl for the amount of carrots you've cooked. Add the rest of the ingredients and stir to coat. Chill for at least 6 hours or overnight.

Yield: Varies

BLACK-EYED PEAS WITH DILL & CAPERS
by Deb Baker (aka Hannah Reed)

Eating black-eyed peas on New Year's Day brings good luck. It's true! And feasting on them any old time gives your feet the beat. It's time for some soul food and nothing compares to this little treat. Besides, black-eyed peas are so good for you.

½ bag of dried blacked-eyed peas, soaked and cooked per directions, with a little sea salt

While that's cooking, mix together:
1 green onion, minced
½ medium onion, chopped
2 tablespoons capers
1 tablespoon dill weed
¾ tablespoon red wine vinegar
2 tablespoons olive oil

In a medium-sized bowl, pour the above ingredients over the cooked black-eyed peas and mix well. (Serve hot or at room temperature.)

Yield: 6 servings

ANDY'S COLESLAW
by Lorraine Bartlett/ LL Bartlett

Andy Rust is **Victoria Square**'s pizza-making king, but he likes to eat other food, too, *and* make use of the area's produce. So it's no wonder he looks forward to fall when he can visit the local farmers' market for home-grown cabbage and carrots, the main ingredients in this lovely coleslaw that will tickle just about everyone's palate.

INGREDIENTS
½ large head cabbage, shredded
2 large carrots, shredded
½ cup finely chopped green pepper
2 tablespoons finely chopped onion

DRESSING
¼ cup sugar
2 tablespoons vinegar
2 tablespoons canola or vegetable oil
1 teaspoon celery seed
¼ teaspoon salt

In a large bowl, combine the cabbage, carrots, green pepper, and onion. In a jar with a tight-sealing lid, combine the dressing ingredients; shake well. Pour the dressing over the cabbage mixture and toss. Cover and chill at least four hours before serving.

Yield: 10 servings

ROASTED BUTTERNUT SQUASH
by Deb Baker (aka Hannah Reed)

Some things are so incredibly easy. Grandma Johnson, from the **Gertie Johnson Backwoods Mysteries,** grows butternuts and gives them away to her friends when they meet up at the church for bingo. Squash is delicious prepared this way, but Grandma doesn't like to do the peeling part now that her eyesight is going. After all, the woman is ninety-two.

INGREDIENTS
1 medium to large butternut squash.
Walnut oil (olive oil works, too)
sea salt to taste

Preheat the oven to 425°. Layer a baking pan with parchment paper. Peel the squash, slice off the ends, scoop out the seeds, and slice into 1-inch thick slices and rings. Drizzle with the oil and use a brush or your hands to distribute the oil evenly on both sides. Sprinkle with sea salt. Bake for 15 minutes, turn the squash, and bake for 15 more minutes. Put the squash under the broiler for a few minutes until brown.

Yield: 4-6 servings

SWEET POTATOES TWO WAYS

by Mary Jane Maffini aka Victoria Abbott

Oh, dear, Jordan Bingham, of the **Book Collector Mysteries,** was raised by her Irish uncles and please don't ask us how they make a living. Let's just say that Jordan is the first person in her family to go straight. She may also be the first in the family to discover food that doesn't come in a can or a package. But even Uncle Mick and Uncle Lucky might tear themselves away from the packaged macaroni and cheese if someone was serving these. Enjoy. Think of all those vitamins.

Classic sweet potato fries

INGREDIENTS
4 sweet potatoes cut into wedges
¼ vegetable oil (Canola rather than olive, as olive oil burns at higher temperatures)
Sea salt

Preheat oven to 450°. Cover a metal baking sheet with aluminum foil. Use two pans if your potatoes are too large. Preheat the baking pan with a very thin coating of oil. Toss the wedges to coat with oil and salt. Place on the baking sheet. Careful–it's really hot! Spread the wedges in a single layer, not too close. Bake for about 30 minutes, flipping with a spatula after 15.

For spicy version: add two tablespoon sugar and two tablespoon chili powder to the oil and salt. You can play with the sweet and spicy proportions to suit yourselves.

Yield: 4 servings

MAIN DISHES

INCREDIBLE CHICKEN

by Kate Collins

This dish really is incredibly tasty and just about the fastest company-worthy entrée to prepare that I've ever found. It's a big hit with the gang at Bloomers Flower Shop, too.

INGREDIENTS
2 chicken breasts, boneless, skinless
¼ cup brown sugar, firmly packed
garlic salt

Preheat the oven to 375°. Arrange the chicken in a lightly oiled baking pan. Season fairly heavily with garlic salt. Sprinkle generously with brown sugar. Bake for 25 minutes. (If the chicken starts to look dry, cover it with foil). May be served hot or cold.

Yield: 2 servings

QUICK AND EASY LEMON CHICKEN
by Leann Sweeney

Jillian Hart, cat lover, widow and amateur sleuth in the *Cats in Trouble Mysteries*, does like to make a nice dinner for her close friend Tom Stewart every now and then. After all, she and the rugged PI and security expert are getting closer now that she is coming to terms with her grief over losing her husband. Not being an accomplished cook, she created this dish that looks fancy, takes little preparation, and is absolutely delicious. Her cats love chicken, but the lemon makes sure they won't be stealing any nibbles. As Jillian knows, cats shy away from citrus. Serve with a chilled white wine, herbed rice, and a side salad, and you'll have a fabulous meal in about thirty minutes!

INGREDIENTS

6 boneless chicken filets, pounded flat with edge of
    a saucer
¼ cup flour
½ teaspoon salt
dash of pepper
3 tablespoons butter
1 cup hot water + 1 chicken bouillon cube -OR- 1
    cup chicken broth
juice of ½ lemon

Combine the flour, salt, and pepper. Coat the filets and save the remaining flour mix. Heat the butter in a frying pan and brown breasts on both sides. Add more butter if needed. Remove the chicken, reduce the heat to low, and add the saved flour, scraping the pan as you stir. Add the bouillon mix/chicken broth and lemon juice. Return the chicken to the pan and simmer for another 5 to 10 minutes. Use the remaining ½ lemon as a garnish by slicing it thin and topping the breasts before serving.

Yield: 6 servings

CHICKEN ROASTED WITH APPLES

by Mary Jane Maffini

If feisty lawyer and victims' rights advocate Camilla MacPhee has had a particularly bad day, her police officer fiancé, Ray Deveau, could easily cheer her up with this fabulous dish. I'm never sure why he's so very nice to her. Wish he'd make it for me while she's off breaking the rules and solving crimes.

INGREDIENTS
2 tablespoons butter
1 chicken (about 4 pounds)
2-4 apples, peeled and diced (about 2 cups). Gala or Fuji or any one of the sweeter varieties
2 tablespoons cider vinegar
½ cup chicken stock
2 bay leaves
1 teaspoon chopped fresh thyme or dried (you can use rosemary instead)
salt and freshly ground pepper

Preheat oven to 350°. Heat butter over medium high heat in a Dutch oven or ovenproof pot large enough to hold the chicken. Brown the chicken on all sides, about 2 minutes a side, until golden. Remove chicken from the pot. Add apples and sauté for 2 minutes or until lightly golden. Add cider vinegar, chicken stock, and bay leaves, and bring to boil. Sprinkle the chicken with thyme, salt and pepper. Bake covered for 60 minutes. Remove the cover and bake for another 15 minutes or until the juices run clear. Remove the bay leaves. Cut up the chicken and serve with the apples and sauce.

Yield: 4 servings

MYSTERY GRILLED CHICKEN STRIPS
by Kate Collins

In the summer, I like quick recipes that work for two people or a crowd. That's why this chicken dish is perfect. It's fast to put together and even faster to grill. It can also be oven baked, and it freezes well. It's a recipe I know my character Abby Knight, from the *Flower Shop Mysteries,* would love for its ease of preparation.

INGREDIENTS
3 skinless chicken breasts cut in long strips
½ cup dry breadcrumbs (I use whole grain panko)
¼ cup Parmesan cheese
1 teaspoon dried thyme
1 teaspoon dried basil
2 tablespoons brown/spicy mustard
2 tablespoons olive oil
¼ teaspoon sea salt
¼ teaspoon sweet smoked paprika (optional)
cooking spray

Preheat the grill (or oven to 400°). Combine the mustard and oil in a shallow bowl and roll the chicken in it. Combine the dry ingredients and spread on a plate or wax paper. Roll chicken strips in the crumb mix. If grilling, arrange the chicken in a single layer on heavy-duty aluminum foil. If oven baking, arrange the breasts on a cookie sheet sprayed with non-stick spray. Grill or bake for approximately 8 minutes or until nicely browned. Serve with your favorite dipping sauce.

Yield: 4 servings

GARLIC CHICKEN

by Mary Jane Maffini

Every once in a while there comes along a recipe that solves a lot of problems. Like garlic chicken. Need to cook for a crowd? Need to make ahead? Need to be able to serve something warm or cold? Need a dish that freezes? This is it. It couldn't be much easier, either!

INGREDIENTS
4-6 chicken breasts, bone in, skin removed
1 cup sour cream
1 tablespoon lemon juice
1 teaspoon Worcestershire sauce
2 peeled cloves garlic
2 slices wheat toast
1 teaspoon sea salt
freshly ground pepper
½ teaspoon Paprika

Preheat oven to 350°. Blend the sour cream, lemon juice, Worcestershire sauce, salt, pepper and paprika in a pie plate. Pulse the toast and garlic in the food processor until nice and "crumby". Dip the chicken in the sour cream mixture, covering generously. Put the chicken in a baking dish. Cover with the crumb mixture. Bake for about forty-five minutes (or more if chicken breasts are thicker). Don't overcook or chicken will be dry. This recipe doubles and triples. It's even better the next day.

Yield: 4 servings

ELLERY'S BEEF BOURGUIGNON

by Ellery Adams

There's only one five-star restaurant in Oyster Bay, North Carolina. Owned by Olivia Limoges, of the **Books By The Bay Mysteries,** The Boot Top Bistro features fine cuisine prepared by Chef Michel. Trained in Paris, Chef Michel created this succulent entrée for The Boot Top's menu, but you could impress all the foodies seated at your dinner table with this dish.

INGREDIENTS
¼ cup all-purpose flour
1 teaspoon salt
½ teaspoon ground black pepper
2 pounds cubed stew meat (cut into bite-sized
     pieces)
4 tablespoons butter
1 onion, chopped
2 carrots, chopped
1 clove garlic, minced
2 cups red wine (Chef Michel prefers a nice Burgundy
     or a pinot noir)
1 cup tomato sauce
1 bay leaf
3 tablespoons fresh parsley, finely chopped
½ teaspoon dried thyme
1 (8 ounce) package of fresh mushrooms, washed,
     dried, and sliced

Preheat the oven to 350°. In a small bowl, combine the flour, salt and ground black pepper. Coat the beef cubes with this mixture. Melt the butter in a large skillet over medium high heat. Add the meat and brown well on all sides. Pour this into a 2-quart casserole dish.

Return the skillet to the heat and add the onion, carrots, and garlic to it. Sauté for approximately 10 minutes, or until the onion is tender. Add the tomato sauce, wine, bay leaf, parsley, and thyme.

Pour over the meat. Bake, covered, for 2½ hours. Remove the cover, add the mushrooms, and bake for 30 more minutes. Remove the bay leaves before serving. If desired, serve over cooked egg noodles.

Yield: 4 servings

POT ROAST IN STROGANOFF SAUCE

by Leann Sweeney

In the **Cats in Trouble Mysteries**, Jillian Hart sells little handmade quilts for cats—and also donates larger quilts she makes to sick children or wounded vets. A day of piecing, quilting and binding means no time for cooking. If Jillian's friends Tom Stewart or Candace Carson are invited for supper, she gets off to an early start by making this easy and different approach to pot roast. Jillian cooks this recipe in the slow cooker on those busy quilting days. Syrah and Merlot, her two boy cats, love the leftovers, but her female Himalayan, Chablis, usually turns up her nose at people food.

INGREDIENTS
4 pounds pot roast (chuck or bottom round)
2 tablespoons canola oil
salt and pepper
1 beef bouillon cube
1 cup water
¼ cup ketchup
1 tablespoon Worcestershire sauce
¼ chopped onion
1 teaspoon caraway seeds
1 (4-ounce) can of sliced mushrooms (Leann leaves
    these out!)
¼ cup flour
½ to ¾ cup sour cream

Season the meat with the salt and pepper and brown in a Dutch oven. Remove. Combine the bouillon, water, ketchup, Worcestershire sauce, onion, and caraway seeds in the pan. Bring to a boil, mashing the bouillon. Return the meat and cover. Simmer, adding more water if necessary, until the meat is fork tender.

Drain the mushrooms, saving the liquid and making sure it's ½ cup. If not, supplement with water. Mix the mushroom liquid and flour. If omitting mushrooms, use ½ cup water instead.

Remove the meat to a platter, add flour/liquid mix to liquid in the Dutch oven, and make gravy. Add the mushrooms and sour cream to this and combine well—do not boil. Spoon a little gravy over the meat.

Serve the meat with noodles or rice and the reserved gravy. If making this in the slow cooker, combine all the sauce ingredients except gravy items in the bottom of the slow cooker. Put the seasoned meat on the top and cook on low, making sure to turn the meat several times to infuse the sauce flavors. Make the gravy in the slow cooker on high.

Yield: 6 servings

ELLERY'S AMAZING OVEN-BARBECUED BRISKET
by Ellery Adams

All of my mysteries take place in the South and one thing Southerners know how to do better than anyone is barbecue a hunk of meat. This is the kind of dish Grumpy and Dixie would fix for their Oyster Bay friends in the *Books by the Bay Mysteries,* and it's wonderful for a summer meal on the patio or a belly-warming entrée in the middle of winter. If you like brisket, then you're going to want to try this!

INGREDIENTS
1 (3-4 pound) beef brisket
1 teaspoon garlic powder
1 teaspoon onion salt
1 teaspoon celery salt
¼ cup apple juice
2 tablespoons Worcestershire sauce
½ teaspoon liquid smoke
Dry rub (Ellery uses Emeril's Original Essence spice)
½ cup store-bought barbecue sauce of your choice
    (Ellery uses KC Masterpiece—Original)

Trim the fat from the brisket. Mix the garlic powder, onion salt, celery salt, apple juice, Worcestershire sauce, and liquid smoke in a small bowl. Using a flavor/marinade injector, inject the liquid mixture into the brisket (at an angle works best). You won't use it all, so discard the rest. Sprinkle the rub generously on the meat and pat it into the surface. Brush on the barbecue sauce (Ellery just spreads it around with her fingers) and wrap the meat in heavy-duty aluminum foil. Place it in a roasting pan and chill for 8 hours.

Bake in a preheated 300° oven for 5 hours or until

a meat thermometer reads 190 degrees. Let stand for 5 to 10 minutes and then cut the brisket on a slant (against the grain) into thin slices. Serve with a small bowl of warmed barbecue sauce on the side.

Yield: 8 servings

BAKED FLOUNDER WITH FRESH LEMON PEPPER
by Leann Sweeney

The Finest Catch is the "fancy" restaurant in small town Mercy, South Carolina, the setting for the *Cats in Trouble Mysteries*. The chef uses fresh fish from nearby Mercy Lake or ocean fish like flounder trucked in from the Gulf Coast. For a special date with her dear friend Tom Stewart (with his dark hair and gorgeous blue eyes), Jillian Hart and Tom head to The Finest Catch. They both love this easy, tasty baked flounder, one of the restaurant's specialties.

INGREDIENTS
grated rind of 3 lemons (should be around 2 tablespoons)
1 tablespoon extra virgin olive oil
1¼ teaspoons coarse black pepper
½ teaspoon salt
2 cloves garlic, minced
4 flounder filets (6-8 ounces each)
cooking spray

Preheat the oven to 425°. Combine the lemon rind, oil, pepper, salt, and garlic in a small bowl. Place the filets flat on a baking pan coated with cooking spray. Spread the lemon pepper mix over each filet and bake 8-10 minutes, or until the fish flakes easily with fork. Garnish with lemon wedges if desired.

Yield: 4 servings

SEAFOOD STEW WITH TOMATOES AND BASIL

by Deb Baker (aka Hannah Reed)

Most of my author friends love to cook as much as I do, but writing takes up a big chunk of our day. When we have a looming deadline, we need simple recipes. This stew is elegant, easy, and fast.

INGREDIENTS
¼ cup olive oil
1 cup onions, chopped
3 cloves of garlic, minced
1½ teaspoons fennel seeds
4 teaspoons oregano
2½ cups crushed or pureed tomatoes
2½ cups clam juice
1 cup dry white wine
2 6½-ounce cans chopped clams, drained but
     reserve liquid
1 6-ounce can crabmeat, drained and liquid tossed
1 pound uncooked shrimp, peeled and deveined
½ cup fresh basil
salt and pepper to taste

Heat the oil. Add the onion, garlic, and spices. Cook until the onion is tender. Add the tomatoes, clam juice, white wine, and liquid from the canned clams. Simmer for 15 minutes. Add the clams, crabmeat, shrimp, and basil. Simmer a few minutes until the shrimp turn opaque. Salt and pepper to taste.

Yield: 4 servings

KATE'S MEATLOAF
by Kate Collins

I see meatloaf as a metaphor for life. Are you the adventurous sort? The rebel in your family? If so, you'll enjoy this version of an old standard. Or are you the kind to play it safe? Personally, I think this recipe makes one heck of a meatloaf. It's healthy, tasty, and spicy.

INGREDIENTS
1 pound ground chuck (or turkey)
½ cup chopped onion
1 teaspoon chili powder
⅓ cup chili sauce
½ teaspoon cinnamon
¼ teaspoon red pepper flakes (or more to make it hotter)
¼ teaspoon black pepper
¼ teaspoon sea salt (or to taste)
½ teaspoon smoked paprika
⅛ teaspoon pepper
¼-½ cup ketchup (organic tastes best)
⅓ cup milk (can also be almond, coconut, or soy milk)
1 egg, beaten slightly
½ cup panko, whole wheat bread crumbs, or oatmeal, or whole grain unsweetened cereal, crushed

Preheat the oven to 350°. Mix all the ingredients. Pour into a shallow baking dish or meat loaf pan. Shape as desired. Bake 1 hour and 15 minutes. Let stand 5 minutes before slicing. Can be frozen.

Yield: 4 servings

SLOW COOKER SPOONABLE LASAGNA
by Leann Sweeney

The **Cats in Trouble Mystery's** Jillian Hart's quilting days are always better when the house smells wonderful, and there's no need to halt the process to fix dinner. Besides, Merlot, her Maine coon cat, is almost as fond of lasagna as Garfield.

INGREDIENTS
1 24-ounce jar of your favorite marinara sauce
2 tablespoons olive oil
1 pound ground beef
1 small onion, chopped
2 cloves garlic minced
1 16-ounce container whole milk ricotta cheese
1 cup shredded Parmesan cheese
1 teaspoon salt
2 cups shredded mozzarella cheese
1 teaspoon oregano
1 10-ounce container refrigerated Alfredo sauce
1 package lasagna noodles-uncooked

Brown the ground beef, onion and garlic in the olive oil. Add the marinara sauce and simmer. Meanwhile, combine the ricotta, Parmesan cheese, salt and oregano. Ladle enough of the prepared sauce in the bottom of the slow cooker to just to cover. Break the lasagna noodles. Place about ⅓ of the package over the sauce. Spoon the cheese mix in globs over the noodles; spoon ⅓ Alfredo sauce over this. Top with a layer of mozzarella and then more sauce. Repeat the layers, ending with a layer of sauce and mozzarella. Cover and cook on low for 8 to 10 hours. It is spoonable the first day, but the second day, after chilled, it can be cut like regular lasagna.

Yield: 6-8 servings

SPECIAL OCCASION FETTUCCINE

by Mary Kennedy

It's not often Lucinda Macavey of the **Dream Club Mysteries** would serve something so outrageously rich. Why, all that butter and cream is practically decadent. But when Lucinda invites a "gentleman caller" to come for dinner, she throws caution to the wind and pulls out all the stops.

INGREDIENTS
1 pound fettuccine noodles, cooked and drained
1 stick (½ cup) butter
1 cup heavy cream
2 cups parmesan cheese, grated
salt and pepper to taste

Melt the butter in a saucepan and carefully add the cream, stirring constantly. Add the grated parmesan cheese. Continue to stir, adding a little salt and pepper to taste. Pour over the cooked noodles and toss gently. Serve immediately.

Yield: 6 servings

ELLERY'S RACK OF LAMB (DIJON MUSTARD STYLE)
by Ellery Adams

Everyone has a favorite condiment. Mine is mustard. And this dish is so easy to prepare and yet so elegant, folks will think you've trained with Chef Michel of the **Books By the Bay Mysteries** when you present them with this rack of lamb. Serve with whole grain rice and steamed asparagus and you'll feel like you're dining at The Boot Top Bistro.

INGREDIENTS
1 rack of lamb, trimmed (3 pounds)
1 cup finely chopped fresh parsley
½ cup Dijon mustard
½ cup breadcrumbs
½ teaspoon freshly ground black pepper
½ teaspoon salt
1 tablespoon fresh rosemary, chopped
1 heaping teaspoon minced garlic

Preheat the oven to 500°. Place the lamb in a large baking pan. Combine the mustard, parsley, salt, pepper, breadcrumbs, and garlic in small bowl. Using your fingers, press the mixture evenly all over the sides of the lamb. Place in the center of the oven and bake for 7 minutes for medium-rare. Allow the lamb to sit for 5 minutes before serving. Garnish with a few sprigs of fresh rosemary.

Yield: 6 servings

VEGETARIAN SHEPHERD'S PIE
by Kate Collins

I've always tried to have one vegetarian meal a week. This is a tasty, satisfying dish that will please everyone's palates, even Abby Knight's finicky cousin Jillian. (***The Flower Shop Mysteries.***)

INGREDIENTS
2 tablespoons extra light olive oil
1 large yellow onion, roughly chopped
4 cloves garlic, crushed
2 tablespoons curry powder
2 teaspoons ground cumin
2 small red or green bell peppers, chopped
1 eggplant, cubed, unpeeled, 3 cups
1 (15-ounce) can diced tomatoes
10 small red potatoes, mashed, or use prepared
    mashed potatoes (see note below)
1 cup frozen peas
½ cup grated Parmesan cheese (or shredded)

Preheat the oven to 400°. Heat 1 tablespoon of the oil in a skillet and add the onion, garlic, curry, and cumin. Sauté until the onions are soft. Transfer to a bowl. Heat the remaining oil in a skillet, add the peppers, eggplant, tomatoes, and ½ cup water. Sauté until soft; about 20 minutes. Stir in the onions. Put in a shallow 8 x 8-inch baking dish. Top with Parmesan cheese. Bake for 15 minutes, then run under the broiler just until the cheese is golden brown.

Yield: 4 servings

Note: You can boil potatoes, drain, mash and add the

half-and-half, peas or use a package of "simply pota-toes" in the refrigerated section of the supermarket.

SPICY WEEK-END ROAST

by Mary Jane Maffini

We haven't grilled this roast outside, but now that we have a grill with a decent thermostat, it's a plan.

INGREDIENTS
1 sirloin tip roast, about 3 pounds
2 tablespoons kosher or sea salt
1 tablespoon sweet paprika
1 tablespoon brown sugar (can use Splenda brown sugar)
3 tablespoons mild New Mexican pepper flakes or 1-2 zippier red pepper flakes.

Preheat your oven to 350°. Mix the dry ingredients and rub all over the roast. You can place the roast in the bowl to do this. It's messy but worth it. Make sure the rub sticks to the meat. Roast for about 45 minutes until a meat thermometer registers medium-rare. Tent the roast (loose foil over it) for about 15 minutes. Of course, you can adjust the times if you like your beef well done. Slice. Be a hero.

Yield: 4 servings

STIR-FRIED VEGGIES AND PASTA

by Lorraine Bartlett/ LL Bartlett

If it were up to the men in her family, Brenda Stanley, of the *Jeff Resnick Mysteries,* knows they'd probably eat steak with fries, seafood with pasta, wash it down with a good Canadian beer, and little else. Therefore, she tries to sneak in veggies whenever she can. Here's a winning recipe to entice people like Jeff and Richard who love pasta any way they can get it. You can make it a meal, or serve it as a side dish (or a dish to pass). No matter how you serve it, you're going to enjoy it.

INGREDIENTS
2 cups uncooked bow-tie pasta
2 medium carrots, julienned
1 medium onion, chopped
2 small zucchini, julienned
1 each medium sweet red, yellow, and green pepper,
    cut into thin strips
1 cup fresh green beans, cut into 1-inch pieces
1 tablespoon olive oil
1 tablespoon sesame oil
2 tablespoons your favorite vinegar
2 tablespoons honey
¼ teaspoon salt
¼ teaspoon chili powder
¼ teaspoon ground ginger

Cook the pasta according to the package instructions. Meanwhile, in a large nonstick skillet or wok, stir-fry the carrots, onions, zucchini, peppers, and beans in hot olive oil for 3-4 minutes or until crisp-tender. Drain the pasta; add to the vegetable mixture. Drizzle with sesame oil. Stir-fry for 2-3 minutes. In a small bowl, combine the vinegar, honey, salt, chili powder, and ginger. Pour over the pasta mixture and toss to coat. Serve immediately.

Yield: 4-6 servings

NORTH WOODS PASTIES

by Deb Baker (aka Hannah Reed)

Pasties (pronounced pass-tees) came to the Upper Peninsula with the coal miners, who ate them for lunch deep underground. This hearty dish can be found in little shops scattered throughout the U.P. The senior citizens in Stonely make the best I've ever had, and after a lot of experimenting, I think I've figured it out. They freeze well so make a bunch. Serve plain, with ketchup, or use your imagination. (This recipe is from the first **Gertie Johnson Backwoods Mystery,** *Murder Grins and Bears It.*)

INGREDIENTS
FOR PASTRY:
3½ cups all-purpose flour
1 teaspoon salt
1 cup butter, cut in pieces
¾ cup ice water
1 egg white

FOR FILLING:
1 pound coarse ground round
1 pound coarse ground pork
1½ cups onions, chopped
1 cup rutabaga, diced
1 cup potatoes, diced
1 teaspoon salt
½ teaspoon pepper
1 tablespoon oil

Preheat the oven to 400°. Sift together 3 cups of the flour and the salt. Cut in the butter until coarse like breadcrumbs. Slowly add ice water until the crumbles become a dough. Shape into a ball, wrap in plastic, and refrigerate for 20 minutes. In a large bowl, combine all the filling ingredients. Grease the baking sheet. Dust your workspace with the remaining flour; divide the dough in 6 pieces and roll each into a circle the size of a dinner plate. On half of each pastie, spread 1 cup of filling. Fold over the dough and crimp the edges. Place the pasties on a baking sheet, cut a few slits in each top, brush with egg white, and bake for 1 hour.

Yield: 6 pasties

VIDALIA ONION QUICHE
by Mary Kennedy

When Etta Mae Beasley brought a treasured family cookbook to a meeting of the Dream Club, Aunt Nadine's recipe for quiche might have been included. Everyone loves it and asks for the recipe. Thank goodness Etta Mae is generous with her recipes.

INGREDIENTS
2 prepared 9-inch pie crusts, uncooked
1 large Vidalia onion
1 cup mayonnaise
4 eggs
1 cup milk
1 pound sharp cheddar cheese, grated
1 tablespoon cornstarch
black pepper to taste

Preheat the oven to 375°. Sauté onion in 1 tablespoon of oil or with cooking spray. Beat the eggs and add mayonnaise, eggs, milk, cheese and cornstarch. Place the sautéed onion into the pie shells. Next, pour the cheese and milk mixture into the pie shells. Bake for 35 minutes or until the top is brown and the quiche has set. This quiche freezes well.

Yield: 8 servings

ELLERY'S HEART-WARMING CHILI

by Ellery Adams

It doesn't get too cold in Oyster Bay, North Carolina, but even the characters from the **Books By the Bay Mysteries** need a warm and filling dish when the winter winds blow off the Atlantic Ocean and chill the residents to the bone. Even Olivia Limoges, who prefers to dine at one of her two restaurants, could whip up this chili in no time. A great dish for football games, snowy days, or to feed a troupe of hungry guests. For fun, serve in bread bowls.

INGREDIENTS
1 pound ground beef
1 onion, finely chopped
2 cloves garlic, finely chopped (or
    1 heaping teaspoon of minced garlic)
1 (14.5 ounce can of chicken broth)
1 (8-ounce) can of tomato sauce (Ellery uses Ragu
    Original)
1 (6-ounce) can of tomato paste
1 (15-ounce) can red kidney beans (you can
        substitute black beans if you'd prefer)
2 teaspoons chili powder
¼ teaspoon ground cumin
⅛ teaspoon ground cinnamon

Cook the beef, onion, and garlic in a large pot until the meat is browned. About 10 minutes. Add the chicken broth, tomato sauce, tomato paste, kidney beans, and spices to the pot. Bring the mixture to a boil and then reduce the heat to low and simmer until thickened. This will take about 20 minutes. Serve with shredded cheese and sour cream.

Yield: 4 servings

RIO GRANDE BEANS & MEATBALLS
by Kate Collins

This simple casserole was my children's favorite dish when they were young. Now they're all grown up and they still love it. If you want to make it healthier, stir in fresh spinach and/or finely chopped carrots.

INGREDIENTS

1 pound ground chuck
¼ cup dry breadcrumbs
1 egg, slightly beaten
1 teaspoon salt (sea salt is best)
2 teaspoons chili powder, divided
⅓ cup chopped onion (large)
1 16-ounce can pork and beans
3 ounces shredded sharp cheddar cheese (or any
    sharp flavored cheese)

Mix ground chuck, breadcrumbs, egg, 1 teaspoon salt, and 1 of the teaspoons chili powder. Shape into large meatballs. Brown in a skillet; pour off the fat. Add the onion to the skillet, sprinkle 1 teaspoon chili powder over the onion. Cover; cook on low for 10 minutes or until the onion is clear. Add the beans. Heat 10 minutes on low, stirring occasionally. Sprinkle the cheese over the top and serve. (Freezes well.)

Yield: 4 servings

SPECIAL SALMON WITH GINGER, SOY AND GARLIC

by Mary Jane Maffini

Fiona Silk, failed romance writer and amateur sleuth in the ***Fiona Silk mysteries,*** hasn't been so lucky in love until recently. There's not much hope she'll ever be able to cook, but her new love. the poet-mechanic Marc-André Paradis, sure knows his way around a kitchen. I can just imagine him making this for Fiona and her sidekicks, Josey and Liz, at his house in the Quebec countryside. Best of all, unlike Fiona's experiments, nothing will blow up or catch fire. This is very easy and good enough for a dinner party. It reheats beautifully in the microwave. But there won't be any leftovers.

INGREDIENTS
4-6 skinless salmon fillets about ¾ inch thick and all
    about the same thickness
Make a marinade with:
4 tablespoons light soy sauce
4 teaspoons fresh ginger (or jarred grated ginger)
2 garlic gloves, crushed through a press
2 teaspoons of dark sesame oil
½ teaspoon sea salt
¼ fresh ground pepper (optional)

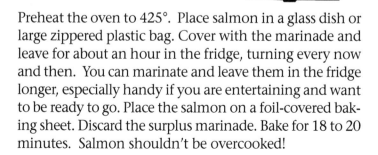

Preheat the oven to 425°. Place salmon in a glass dish or large zippered plastic bag. Cover with the marinade and leave for about an hour in the fridge, turning every now and then. You can marinate and leave them in the fridge longer, especially handy if you are entertaining and want to be ready to go. Place the salmon on a foil-covered baking sheet. Discard the surplus marinade. Bake for 18 to 20 minutes. Salmon shouldn't be overcooked!

Yield: 4-6 servings

ELLERY'S BLACK BEAN BURGERS

by Ellery Adams

The Bayside Crab House features dozens of succulent seafood dishes on its menu, but it also offers pasta and entrees for its vegetarian patrons. Hudson Salter's black bean burgers are tender and tasty and that little dash of jalapeño pepper transforms them from a plain old burger to a gourmet delight.

INGREDIENTS
1 15-ounces can black beans, drained
1 small onion, chopped
1 tablespoon finely chopped jalapeño pepper
¼ cup breadcrumbs
1 egg, beaten
½ cup shredded cheddar cheese
2 cloves fresh garlic, minced
¼ teaspoon pepper
¼ cup vegetable oil

In a large bowl, mash the black beans. Mix in the onion, jalapeño pepper, crushed breadcrumbs, beaten egg, cheese, and pepper. Divide into 4 equal parts. Shape into patties. Heat the vegetable oil in a large, non-stick skillet over medium-high heat. Fry the patties until golden, about 6 to 8 minutes per side. Top with cheese slices and/or a splash of taco sauce.

Yield: 4 servings

CHICKPEAS IN TOMATO SAUCE WITH FETA AND WINE

by Kate Collins

This is an easy one-pan meal that's great as a sauce over rice or pasta, or ladled over meat, such as beef or pork.

INGREDIENTS
1½ tablespoons olive oil
1 small onion chopped
2 cloves garlic, minced
1 tablespoons dried oregano
1 14-ounce can diced tomatoes (reserve juice; I used Italian spiced tomatoes)
2 cups dry white wine
1 15-ounce can chickpeas (garbanzo beans) drained
¾ cup crumbled feta cheese
ground pepper to taste

Heat the oil in medium saucepan over medium heat. Stir in the onions, garlic and oregano. Cook and stir about 10 minutes until the onions are clear. Mix in the tomatoes and heat through. Mix in the wine and continue to simmer for about 15 minutes, until thickened.

Stir in the beans, feta, and remaining tomato juice and cook 5 minutes, until the cheese has melted. Season with the pepper as desired. Allow to cool 5 minutes before serving. (If desired, the beans can be mashed to make a thick, smooth sauce.)

Yield: 4 servings

CROCKPOT MACARONI AND CHEESE
by Mary Kennedy

When Dr. Maggie moved from Manhattan to Florida in the **Talk Radio Mysteries**, she discovered a cute little café that served Mac N Cheese. It quickly became her favorite and she hopes you will love it, too.

INGREDIENTS

2 cups uncooked elbow macaroni (or whatever shape pasta you like)
4 tablespoons butter
10 ounces sharp cheddar cheese, grated (about 2½ cups)
½ cup sour cream
1 can (10.75-ounces) condensed cheddar cheese soup
1 cup milk
½ teaspoon dry mustard
½ teaspoon black pepper

Boil the macaroni until cooked, then drain. Melt the butter and grated cheese in a saucepan, stirring constantly. Place the butter/cheese mixture in greased crockpot and add all the other ingredients. Stir well. Cook for 3 hours on low, stirring now and then.

Yield: 8-10 servings

ELLERY'S PANCETTA AND GRUYERE TART
by Ellery Adams

In the first **Charmed Pie Shoppe Mystery,** Ella Mae LeFaye is baking up a storm. Pies, tarts, and quiches come out of her kitchen all day long and each one is filled with a touch of magic. She serves her customers this savory tart along with a generous side salad. There's nothing quite like the blend of creamy cheese and the salty crunch of pancetta (think Italian bacon) to enjoy at a Sunday brunch or as a light supper.

INGREDIENTS
butter and flour for prepping tart pan
1 pie crust (store bought or homemade)
2 teaspoons vegetable oil
3 ounces pancetta or any other type of bacon, cut into small pieces
5 eggs, lightly beaten
½ cup mascarpone cheese, at room temperature
2 cups shredded Gruyere cheese
3 green onions, thinly sliced
½ teaspoon ground pepper
Charmed egg wash:
1 egg yolk
1 tablespoon half and half

Preheat the oven to 400°. Butter and flour the bottom and sides of a 9-inch tart pan. Place a piecrust in the tart pan. Carefully press the crust into the bottom and sides of the pan. Trim excess crust using kitchen scissors. With the tines of a fork, prick the pastry in three places. Using a pastry brush, coat the crust with the Charmed egg wash. (To achieve a golden brown color for your crust, brush the surface with 1 tablespoon half and half and 1 large egg yolk.)

Put the pan on a baking sheet and bake for 10 minutes or until the egg wash has set. Allow the crust to cool. In a medium skillet, heat the oil. Add the pancetta and cook until brown and crispy (like regular bacon). This will take 8-10 minutes. Transfer to a plate covered with a layer of paper towels. Let drain.

In a medium-sized mixing bowl, combine the beaten eggs, mascarpone cheese, Gruyere cheese, green onions, pepper, and pancetta. Mix gently. Pour filling into the piecrust and bake until the mixture has set and the top has a nice, golden bark, 18-20 minutes. Cool the tart for 15 minutes before removing from the tart pan.

Yield: 6-8 servings

PICADILLO MEATLOAF/BURGERS
by Kate Collins

Because Picadillo isn't made as a loaf, but rather a loose mixture. I adapted my recipe by taking out the water. After I had it mixed, I decided to make burgers, so I took out the tomato paste, shaped the meat mixture into 5 patties, slapped them on my Foreman grill and - OH, WOW! Talk about a de-lish dish! And perfect for Fourth of July barbeques.

So here it is if you want to give this Cuban-inspired entrée a try, use super lean ground beef, ground turkey or chicken, and make it as a meatloaf, burger, or, if you want to make it in the traditional way (sloppy Joe style) add in 3 tablespoons of tomato paste, enough water to make it sloppy, then sauté the entire mix until meat the is cooked, and serve it over yellow rice or on buns. Versatile, isn't it?

INGREDIENTS
1 pound super lean ground beef, or ground turkey or chicken
1 tablespoon extra virgin olive oil
1 small onion, minced
1 large clove garlic, minced
½ red, yellow, or green bell pepper, minced
3 teaspoons chili powder
1½ teaspoons oregano
1½ teaspoons cumin
½ teaspoon cinnamon
¼ cup chopped pitted olives—any type
1 tablespoons capers, rinsed
3 tablespoons tomato paste (meatloaf only)

Sauté the onion, garlic, and pepper until softened. Mix into the meat with the rest of the ingredients.

Shape into meatloaf or individual burgers. Grill the burgers until pink in the center—or bake the meatloaf at 350° for an hour or until the top looks brown.

Yield: 4 servings

PIES, CAKES & OTHER SWEETS

PETE'S PECAN PIE
by Maggie Sefton

This recipe for pecan pie is one of my family favorites. I've made it for family occasions for years— Thanksgiving, Christmas, and whenever we wanted a super-rich delicious dessert. Our family has always been big on pies. I developed this particular version by tinkering with several different recipes until I got the flavor I liked. You can make it with or without the addition of bourbon or rum. No matter which way you choose, it's yummy. Since Pete is the owner and chief cook/chef in Pete's Porch Café, which is part of the **Kelly Flynn Knitting Mysteries,** I decided to give Pete my Pecan pie recipe. He deserves it. Enjoy!

INGREDIENTS
3 large eggs
⅔ cup dark brown sugar, firmly packed
dash of salt
1 cup dark corn syrup
⅓ cup melted butter (no substitutions)
1-2 tablespoons bourbon or rum (if desired)
1½-2 cups pecan halves

Beat the eggs thoroughly with the brown sugar and salt, then add the corn syrup and ⅓ cup melted butter. Beat until well mixed, and then add the bourbon or rum. Add pecan halves. Pour into a 9-inch unbaked pie shell (see recipe below).

Bake in a moderate (350°) oven for 50 minutes or until a knife inserted in the center comes out clean. Cool on a wire rack.

Yield: 1 pie

Butter Crust Pastry (makes one unbaked 9-inch pie
    crust)
1½ level cups all-purpose flour
1 stick (½ cup) butter, cold
1½ teaspoons salt (as desired)
4 or 5 tablespoons cold water

Measure the flour into a mixing bowl and stir in the
salt. Mix well. Cut in cold butter with a pastry blender
or two knives. The mixture should be coarse and
crumbly. Gradually sprinkle in the cold water, mixing
well with a fork until all dry ingredients are moistened. Form the pastry into a large ball. Lightly flour
the rolling surface (pastry cloth, wax paper, or other)
and rolling pin. Roll the dough into a circle wider
than a glass pie plate, so there is at least a 1-2 inches
of crust overhang. Fit the crust into the pie plate, trim
the overhang, and flute the edge of crust as desired.

   This recipe allows for an ample amount of pastry.
Do not be concerned if the pastry tears when trying to
remove from the rolling surface. Butter crust is light
and delicate and tears easily, but is also easily repaired.
Fit the crust into pie plate and "seam" together the
torn pieces by dipping a finger into cold water and
lightly brushing across the edges. The edges will disappear when baked, and that same delicate fragile
quality of the pastry when handling is responsible for
the melt-in-your-mouth flakiness of the butter crust.
Enjoy!

ELLERY'S CHOCOLATE BOURBON PECAN PIE
by Ellery Adams

Coming up with recipes for the **Charmed Pie Shoppe Mysteries** was a delight. The buttery scents of baking crust combined with the aromas of browning pecans and melted chocolate will make your kitchen as enchanted as Ella Mae's. Make one pie for yourself and give one to a friend or loved one. This pie travels well and tastes wonderful with a cup of coffee.

INGREDIENTS
1 box refrigerated pie crusts (Ellery prefers Pillsbury)
¾ cup granulated sugar
1 cup light corn syrup
½ cup salted butter
4 eggs, beaten
2 tablespoons bourbon
1 teaspoon vanilla extract
6 ounces semisweet chocolate chips
1 cup chopped pecans

Preheat the oven to 325°. In a medium saucepan combine the sugar, corn syrup, and butter. Cook over medium heat, stirring constantly, until the butter melts and the sugar dissolves. Cool slightly. In a large bowl blend the eggs, bourbon, and vanilla. Mix well. Slowly pour the sugar mixture into the egg mixture, whisking constantly. Stir in the chocolate chips and pecans. Pour the mixture into the pie shells. Bake for 50 to 55 minutes or until you spot a lovely golden bark.

Yield: 2 pies

KAREN'S FAMOUS LEMON ICEBOX PIE
by Leann Sweeney

In the **Cats in Trouble Mysteries**, Karen Stewart is the mother of Jillian Hart's love interest Tom. She won Jillian's heart with this dessert the first time she was invited to eat supper at Karen's cute little retro house in Mercy, South Carolina in the very first book in the series, *The Cat, The Quilt and The Corpse.* Karen is an odd bird—flighty and quirky—but she knows her way around a Southern kitchen. There are plenty of Lemon Icebox Pie recipes out there, but this one is the best Jillian has ever tasted.

INGREDIENTS
1½ cup cookie crumbs — preferably lemon, but
     vanilla wafers will do
½ cup finely chopped almonds
¾ stick of butter (6 tablespoons)
¼ cup granulated sugar
¼ cup heavy cream
1 cup confectioners' sugar
6 ounces cream cheese, softened
½ cup sour cream
8 ounces heavy cream beaten with sugar to taste—
     not too sweet
1 3½ ounce box instant lemon pie filling
1¾ cup milk
1 teaspoon lemon juice
1 teaspoon lemon rind, grated
2 cups Cool Whip topping or heavy cream beaten
     and sweetened
¼ cup hard lemon candy

Preheat the oven to 300°. Combine the finely crushed

cookie crumbs, almonds, butter, sugar and heavy cream together. Pat in the bottom and up the sides of a 9-inch pie pan. Bake for 15 minutes. Set aside to cool.

FILLING:

Mix the confectioners' sugar, softened cream cheese, sour cream, and whipped topping until smooth and creamy. Spread in the bottom of the cooled crust. Mix the lemon pie mix according to package directions, with the milk, lemon juice, and grated lemon rind. Spread over the cream cheese layer in the crust. Refrigerate for about 1 hour.

Top with whipped topping or whipped cream and sprinkle crushed lemon candies as decoration. Keep refrigerated.

Yield: 6-8 slices

ELLERY'S BANANA PUDDIN' PIE
by Ellery Adams

Everyone's had a bunch of bananas on the counter that are in danger of spoiling before they can be eaten. To Ella Mae LeFaye, of the **Charmed Pie Shoppe Mysteries,** this problem presented an opportunity to create a new pie. This smooth, creamy, delicious pie is sure to be a favorite with banana lovers.

INGREDIENTS
1 pie crust (homemade or store bought)
¼ cup cold water
2¼ teaspoon (1 package) unflavored gelatin
2 cups whole milk
¼ cup cornstarch
4 large egg yolks
⅔ cup sugar
¼ teaspoon salt
1 teaspoon vanilla extract
3 large, very ripe bananas, peeled and sliced

FOR WHIPPED TOPPING:
1 cup heavy cream
2 tablespoons confectioners' sugar
1 teaspoon dark rum
1 teaspoon vanilla extract

GARNISH:
6 ounces semisweet chocolate, shaved into curls using a vegetable peeler.

Transfer the dough to a 9-inch pie pan. Trim and flute the edge. Using a fork, pierce the dough several times, then line with aluminum foil and freeze for 30 minutes.

Preheat the oven to 450°. Place the dough-lined pan on a baking sheet and fill the foil with pie weights. Bake for 12 to 15 minutes. Cool and then remove the foil and weights. Pour cold water into a small bowl and add the gelatin. Let the gelatin firm up for about 10 minutes.

Next, pour the milk into a medium saucepan and warm over low-medium heat until hot (about 10 minutes), but don't allow it to boil. In a large bowl, whisk the egg yolks and sugar. Add the cornstarch and salt and blend until there are no lumps. Gradually add the hot milk to the egg mixture, stirring constantly. Add the gelatin to the mix and blend thoroughly. Return entire mixture to saucepan.

Cook over medium heat until the mixture begins to bubble, whisking constantly. Remove from the heat and immediately add the vanilla. Line the banana slices along the cooled piecrust and then spread the custard on top. Put a piece of plastic wrap directly onto the surface of the filling, piercing the plastic a few times with a knife. Cover and refrigerate for 2 to 4 hours.

To make the whipped topping, place a large stainless steel bowl and blender beaters in the freezer for 10 minutes. Remove from the freezer and then add the cream, rum, vanilla, and sugar into the chilled bowl. Beat on high speed until stiff peaks form. Spread the topping over chilled pie and garnish with chocolate shavings.

Yield: 6-8 servings

RUTH'S BLUEBERRY PIE

by Maggie Sefton

When I wrote the scene in *Needled To Death*, the second in the **Kelly Flynn Knitting Mysteries,** where Kelly visits Curt and Ruth Stackhouse, I envisioned them enjoying one of my very favorite pies—blueberry. So, I gave Ruth Stackhouse my "down home" pie recipe for an all-American favorite. Enjoy—and don't forget the vanilla ice cream!

BUTTER CRUST PASTRY (See page 76)

BLUEBERRY PIE FILLING
⅓ cup all-purpose flour
½ cup granulated sugar
dash cinnamon
1 teaspoon freshly grated lemon rind
1 teaspoon freshly squeezed lemon juice
4 cups fresh blueberries
2-3 tablespoons butter

Preheat the oven to 425°. Prepare the butter crust pastry. Mix the flour, sugar, cinnamon, and lemon rind in medium bowl. Sprinkle lemon juice over the blueberries and stir into the mixture. Pour into the pastry-lined pie pan. Dot with butter and cover with lattice piecrust top.

Lattice piecrust top: Place 6-8 strips across fruit filling. Take the cross strip and weave it through other strips, starting in the center. Fold the strips back as needed. Continue weaving the lattice until desired result is obtained. Trim the edges of strips on lattice crust and fold lower overhanging pastry crust edge up and over. Seal the edges and flute with a fork.

Cover the edges with a 3-inch strip of baking foil to keep from burning (remove foil for the last 15 minutes of baking). Bake until crust is lightly browned and the juices bubbling, approximately 35 to 45 minutes.

Note: Oven temperatures vary. Check the pie after 30 minutes and continue accordingly.

Yield: 6-8 servings

BEER CAKE

by Lorraine Bartlett/ LL Bartlett

They say the way to a man's heart is through his stomach, and my character, Katie Bonner, the protagonist in my **Victoria Square Mystery series,** is always looking for ways to melt her guy's heart. Let's be honest, most guys love beer, so they're all sure to love this cake.

INGREDIENTS
1 cup shortening
2 cups brown sugar, firmly packed
2 eggs
3 cups sifted flower
½ teaspoon salt
½ teaspoon baking soda
½ teaspoon ground cloves
½ teaspoon allspice
½ teaspoon cinnamon
2 cups beer
1 cup chopped walnuts
2 cups chopped dates
confectioners' sugar (optional)

Preheat the oven to 350°. Cream the shortening, brown sugar, and eggs until fluffy. Add the beer. Sift the flour and other dry ingredients. Slowly add to the wet ingredients. Fold in the walnuts and dates until just mixed. Pour batter into a tube or Bundt pan. Bake for 75 to 80 minutes. Remove from the oven and cool for at least 10 minutes before removing from the pan. If desired, dust with confectioners' sugar.

Yield: 8-12 servings

GRANDMA ROSIE'S CHERRY LOAF CAKE
by Kate Collins

The holidays wouldn't be special without my mother's famous cherry loaf cake. This simple, pretty dessert has been a family favorite for forty years. Named after my mom, it was the cake she always brought to our big Thanksgiving dinners, and what all the grandchildren would request on their birthdays, even after my nephew sneezed on his cake before he blew out his candles, sending confectioners' sugar flying into the faces of everyone gathered at the table. We always think of Mom when we make it.

INGREDIENTS
1 package yellow cake mix— with pudding in the mix
1 21-ounce can cherry pie filling
confectioners' sugar

Prepare the cake mix according to package directions (you can substitute walnut, coconut, or canola oil for the vegetable oil), but reduce the water to ½ cup. Spread the batter in greased 13 x 9-inch pan. Spoon the pie filling on top of the batter. Using a spatula, fold the filling into the batter just enough to give it a marbled look. Bake for 55 to 60 minutes or until the cake tests done by springing back when lightly touched in center. Cool. Sprinkle with confectioners' sugar.

Yield: 20-24 servings

SOUTH OF THE BORDER CAKE
by Leann Sweeney

When quilter Jillian Hart, the kindhearted, cat loving main character in the **Cats in Trouble Mysteries**, left Texas for South Carolina, she brought a few of her grandmother's recipes with her. Jillian would help her grandma make this cake when they needed to bring dessert to the potluck dinner at church. Jillian likes an easy recipe and this cake always has folks asking for another piece.

INGREDIENTS
1 20-ounce can crushed pineapple in pineapple
   juice (do not drain)
2 teaspoons baking soda
2 eggs, beaten
2 cups all-purpose flour
1 cup chopped walnuts or pecans
2 cups granulated sugar

Preheat the oven to 350°. Combine all ingredients and mix well. Pour the batter into a lightly greased 13 x 9-inch pan. Bake for 40 to 45 minutes.

WHILE THE CAKE IS BAKING, COMBINE:
1 8-ounce package cream cheese
2 cups confectioners' sugar
1 stick (½ cup) of butter, melted
1 teaspoon vanilla extract

Ice the warm cake and when completely cool, refrigerate and store in the refrigerator.

Yield: 8 servings

ELLERY'S CHOCOLATE MOCHA CAKE
by Ellery Adams

This is one of those cakes that you dream about eating. If you like the flavor of coffee combined with a cake so moist that it'll stick to your fork, then this is a dream-come-true cake for you. It's the perfect accompaniment to an afternoon spent reading while sheets of rain pour down outside. It's also the kind of cake you'll want to take to bake sales, family gatherings, or serve at a birthday party. Enjoy with a cold glass of milk.

INGREDIENTS
2 cups cake flour
2 cups granulated sugar
⅔ cup unsweetened cocoa powder
½ cup vegetable oil
2 eggs
1 cup buttermilk
2 teaspoons baking soda
½ teaspoon salt
1 teaspoon baking powder
3 tablespoons instant coffee powder
1 cup hot water

Preheat the oven to 350°. Grease two 9-inch cake pans. Measure the flour, sugar, cocoa, oil, eggs, buttermilk, baking powder, baking soda, and salt into a mixing bowl. Dissolve the instant coffee in hot water. Add to the mixing bowl. Beat at medium speed for 2 minutes until smooth; the batter will be thin. Pour into the prepared pans.

Bake for 35 minutes, or until a toothpick comes out clean. Cool in pans for 10 minutes, and then turn out onto racks to cool completely. Frost with coffee icing. For the garnish, sprinkle the outside edges of cake with the dark chocolate shavings.

COFFEE ICING
4 cups confectioners' sugar
½ cup unsalted butter, softened
6 tablespoons strong brewed coffee
2 teaspoons vanilla extract

Beat together the sugar, butter, coffee, and vanilla until smooth. To thicken the frosting, add more confectioners' sugar.

Yield: 8-10 slices

CRANBERRY ORANGE NUT BREAD

by Maggie Sefton

This nut bread is good all year round, not just during the holiday season. Again, I kept tinkering with recipes until I came up with the flavors that I especially like. I simply love the flavor of orange in this rich quick bread. It's quick to make, and cranberries can usually be found year round. (If not, try one of the larger grocery chain stores.) Give it a try and enjoy!

INGREDIENTS
2 cups all-purpose flour
1½ teaspoons baking powder
½ teaspoon baking soda
1 teaspoon ground cinnamon
½ teaspoon salt
1½ cups granulated sugar
1 cup orange juice
¼ cup melted butter
2 eggs
1 cup fresh cranberries (not frozen)
1 cup chopped walnuts
½ cup grated orange peel

Preheat the oven to 350°. Grease one regular size bread loaf pan (or two small loaf pans). Dust the pan lightly with flour, dumping the excess. Combine the flour, baking powder, baking soda, cinnamon, and salt in large mixing bowl. Combine the sugar, orange juice, melted butter, and eggs in another bowl, mixing well. Stir into flour mixture along with cranberries, walnuts, and orange rind. Mix well, blending all ingredients. Pour into the prepared loaf pan.

Bake for 50 minutes or until a knife inserted into

the center of the loaf comes out clean. Remove the pan to a wire rack to cool for 10 minutes, then run the knife around the edges of the pan and turn out onto a wire rack to cool completely.

Yield: 1 loaf (12-16 slices)

good

ELLERY'S DARK CHOCOLATE BANANA BREAD
by Ellery Adams

This is the best bread to make if you have a girlfriend coming over for a cup of coffee. The soft bananas combined with the richness of the dark chocolate baked in a cushion of moist bread will have even the most tight-lipped of characters confessing everything! If only Chief Rawlings of the Oyster Bay Police Department (in the **Books By The Bay Mysteries**) had this bread on hand for his interrogations, there'd by no more crime in his seaside town.

INGREDIENTS

2 cups all-purpose flour
2 teaspoons baking powder
4½ ounces butter (1 stick plus 1 tablespoon), soft
    enough for mixing
1 cup superfine sugar
4 ripe bananas, good and smashed
    (Ellery likes to use her fists!)
2 eggs, beaten
1 teaspoon vanilla extract
1 cup dark chocolate chips

Preheat the oven to 350°. Sift the flour and baking powder into a large bowl. Mix the butter, sugar, bananas, eggs, and vanilla extract in a medium bowl. Add the chocolate chips. Add to the flour mixture and stir to combine. Do not over mix. Ellery likes to fold the dough carefully until just mixed. This makes the bread light and airy. Pour the batter into a lightly greased and floured 8 x 4-inch loaf pan and bake for 1 hour and 15 minutes, or until a toothpick inserted into center comes out clean. Cool in the pan before turning out onto a wire rack.

Yield: 1 loaf (12-16 slices)

*used 2 pans
mine weren't
tor deep*

PUMPKIN NUT BREAD

by Maggie Sefton

I love practically all nut breads, and I love the flavor of pumpkin. So, this nut bread is a natural favorite for me, especially when you add in the spices. Cinnamon, cloves, allspice, cardamom—are a wonderful heady rich combination and engage the senses. No wonder they are used in so many holiday recipes. But those same spices are wonderful all year round. Enjoy!

INGREDIENTS
2 cups all-purpose flour
1 cup light or golden brown sugar, firmly packed
1 tablespoon baking powder
1 teaspoon ground cinnamon
¼ teaspoon salt
¼ teaspoon baking soda
¼ teaspoon ground nutmeg
¼ teaspoon ground cloves
1 cup canned pumpkin
½ cup milk
2 eggs, slightly beaten
⅓ cup butter
½ cup chopped walnuts (more if desired)

Preheat the oven to 350°. In a large mixing bowl, combine 1 cup of the flour, then add the brown sugar, baking powder, cinnamon, salt, baking soda, nutmeg, and cloves. Add the pumpkin, milk, eggs, and butter. Beat with an electric mixer or by hand with a wooden spoon until well-blended; at least two minutes. Add the remaining flour and beat well. Stir in the nuts.

Pour the batter into a greased 9 x 5-inch loaf pan. Bake for 60 to 65 minutes or until a knife inserted near the center comes out clean. Cool for 10 minutes on a wire rack. Remove from the pan and cool completely on a wire rack. Wrap and store in the refrigerator at least overnight before slicing.

Yield: 1 loaf (12-16 slices)

CAPE BRETON 'PORK' PIES
by Mary Jane Maffini

Cape Breton is a gorgeous island on the east coast of Canada. It has a strong Scottish heritage and you can still find Gaelic signs. In the way of Cape Bretoners, these are not pies, nor do they contain pork. Instead they are darling little tarts with shortbread pastry filled with dates, brown sugar and lemon, topped with old-fashioned butter icing. An inside joke, I suppose. Growing up in Cape Breton back in the day back when mothers were known for their baking, they were the thing to bring to a party. I couldn't do that, because my mother didn't know how to make them. My mother was a gifted cook, but a 'come-from-away'. She never truly understood what was going on with Cape Breton Pork Pies. It took a lot of sleuthing for me to track down and put together this recipe many years later using heritage cookbooks and experimentation. They are a bit of work, but worth every minute.

TART SHELLS (MAKES 24):
1 cup butter
4 tablespoons icing sugar
2 cups flour

Cut the butter into the flour; add the sugar and knead until well-blended. Press small amounts of dough into small muffin tins. Bake at 425 % for about eight minutes. They shouldn't brown.

FILLING:
2 cups chopped dates
1 ½ cups brown sugar

1 cup water
juice of one lemon

Simmer ingredients until soft. Cool and fill tart shells.

Old-fashioned butter icing: Blend together 1 ½ cups icing sugar and ¼ cup soft butter. Add 2 tablespoon cream (or soft cream cheese) and vanilla and almond flavouring to taste. Decorate tops of cooled, filled tarts. Eat.

BLUEBERRY STREUSEL COFFEE CAKE
by Lorraine Bartlett/ LL Bartlett

Don't you just love the summer when so many wonderful fruits and vegetables are in season? So does
Katie Bonner of the **Victoria Square Mysteries**. Oh,
it's winter (spring or fall)? Not to worry—frozen blueberries work well in this recipe, too. Just don't thaw
them before you add them to the batter, or you'll
have a blue cake. But even if you did—it would still
taste just as good.

INGREDIENTS
2 cups all-purpose flour
¾ cup sugar
2 teaspoons baking powder
¼ teaspoon salt
1 egg
½ cup milk
½ cup butter, softened
1 cup fresh or frozen blueberries
1 cup chopped pecans or walnuts

STREUSEL TOPPING:
½ cup sugar
⅓ cup all-purpose flour
¼ cup cold butter

Preheat the oven to 375°. In a large bowl, combine
the flour, sugar, baking powder, and salt. Whisk the
egg, milk, and butter; stir into the dry ingredients.
Fold in the blueberries and nuts. Spread into a greased
9-inch square baking pan.

   For the topping, combine the sugar and flour into
a bowl; cut in the butter until crumbs form. Sprinkle

the topping over the cake batter. Bake for 35 to 40 minutes or until a toothpick inserted into the center comes out clean. Cool on a wire rack.

Yield: 9 servings

BLISSFUL LIME CREAM CHEESE PIE
by Mary Kennedy

Vera Mae Atkins, of the **Talk Radio Mysteries,** says it is "sheer bliss" to come home after a hard day at the radio station and have a slice of this pie. And it's quick to make. Vera Mae uses limes from her garden. It's one of the advantages of living in sunny Florida.

INGREDIENTS
1 8-ounce package cream cheese
1 14-ounce can condensed milk
1 8-ounce container frozen whipped topping, thawed
½ cup lime juice
1 graham-cracker crust

Soften the cream cheese, mix with the condensed milk. Fold in the whipped topping and lime juice. Pour into the crust. Refrigerate and serve cold.

Yield: 8 servings

THE WORLD'S BEST STRAWBERRY PIE

by Mary Kennedy

Irina Yaslov from the **Talk Radio Mysteries** says the way to a man's heart is through his stomach. She discovered this pie at a popular restaurant chain when she first came to the US.

INGREDIENTS
1 cup sugar
2 tablespoons cornstarch
1 cup water
1 teaspoon lemon juice
¼ cup strawberry gelatin powder
1 ½ quarts strawberries, sliced
1 pie shell, baked

Combine the sugar, cornstarch, and water in saucepan. Cook over medium heat until thickened and clear, stirring constantly. Add the lemon juice and gelatin. Place the strawberries in the baked pie shell. Pour the cooled liquid mixture over the strawberries and chill in the refrigerator. If desired, top with whipped cream.

Yield: 8 servings

BEST AND EASIEST ICE CREAM CAKE
by Mary Jane Maffini

This is our traditional summer birthday cake at chez Maffini. Everyone loves it and there are lots of us of all ages. You can mess with the ingredients and the proportions and because you don't bake it, it's hard to go wrong. It's more of a way of life than a recipe. We often decorate it with fresh strawberries and for evening parties we serve it just after dark with lots of lit sparklers.

INGREDIENTS
Cookie crumb base (see below)
Your favorite combo of ice cream (at least two flavors, preferably with a color contrast and flavors that will harmonize
Whipping cream for icing
Confectioner's sugar
Kahlua or other liqueur

FOR CRUST:
Preheat oven to 350°
1½ cups chocolate cookie crumbs
6 tablespoons butter, melted in microwave
3 tablespoons sugar
2 tablespoons liqueur (chocolate, coffee flavor, or whatever you love or have on hand)

Mix the cookie crumbs, sugar, melted butter and liqueur. Press into the bottom of 10-inch round springform pan. Bake for 6-8 minutes. Chill. Can't stand the heat? Just make your favorite unbaked cookie crumb crust.

FILLING:

1½ quarts (in total) of your two favorite compatible ice cream flavors. (We love Dutch chocolate for one layer and French vanilla with chocolate sprinkles for the other. It's wonderful with coffee ice cream and cappuccino duet too. Mix 'em up to suit yourselves.)

4 tablespoons liquor. (You can use rum, whiskey or bourbon if you want. It's best if you use a different flavor from the crust. Don't want liqueur? Leave it out. We don't put it in the children's version.)

TOPPING:

½ cup chilled whipping cream

1 teaspoon. espresso powder or 2 teaspoons cocoa powder. (Or both. If these don't go with your ice cream flavors, try vanilla extract or almond extract.)

1 tablespoon Confectioners' sugar

Filling: soften the darker of the two ice creams while the crust is cooking. Add 2 tablespoons of liqueur if using. Spread over the chilled crust and freeze for at least one hour. Soften the second ice cream container and blend in remaining 2 tablespoons of liqueur. Spread over the darker ice cream. Chill for one hour. Whip the cream with cocoa or espresso powder (or whatever flavor you've chosen) If you're not driving, toss in a bit more liqueur. Smooth over the top of ice cream like icing. (You can omit this step and put whipped cream and fruit on top if you prefer.) Sprinkle with chocolate shavings or your favorite cake toppers. Try chocolate covered espresso beans or fresh strawberries or raspberries depending on the flavor of your ice creams. Wrap well and freeze at least two hours or overnight. Remove from the freezer about fifteen minutes before serving. Remove from the springform pan and transfer to a cake plate. It can be tricky to get the crust off the bottom and you may need a sharp knife for that. Don't leave fingerprints. (Ask me sometime about the time the cake shot across the screened porch. First, make sure I have a strong drink in my hand.)

Yield: 8-10 servings

KAHLUA CAKE

by Mary Kennedy

This is one of Dr. Maggie's favorite desserts and she serves it to all her friends in Cypress Grove in the ***Talk Radio Mysteries.***

INGREDIENTS
1 box dark chocolate cake mix
1 pint sour cream
1 small box instant vanilla pudding
6 ounces semi-sweet chocolate chips
4 large eggs
¾ cup Kahlua
¼ cup cooking oil

Pre-heat the oven to 350°. Spray a Bundt pan with non-stick baking spray. Mix all the ingredients except chocolate chips. Fold in the chocolate chips and pour the mixture into the Bundt pan. Bake for 60 minutes, but check at 55 minutes. Cake is done when a toothpick comes out clean. Let the cake cool before inverting it onto a plate.

Yield: 12 servings

TRUTH OR DARE
CHOCOLATE CHIP CAKE

by Mary Kennedy

Vera Mae Atkins from the **Talk Radio Mysteries** makes this cake whenever anyone at WYME Radio has a birthday. She says she can't remember why it's called Truth or Dare Cake but everyone loves it. There are two versions, a yellow cake and a chocolate one.

INGREDIENTS

1 box yellow cake mix (Vera Mae uses Duncan Hines Golden Butter flavor)

1 box instant vanilla pudding

1 cup sour cream

1 cup cooking oil

4 eggs

½ cup water

1 cup regular semi-sweet chocolate chips, and 1 cup "mini" chocolate chips

Preheat the oven to 350°. In a large bowl, combine the cake mix, pudding mix, sour cream, cooking oil, eggs, and water. Add chocolate chips. Pour into a Bundt pan. Bake for 50 minutes. Cool before inverting onto a platter. For the "all-chocolate" version of this cake, simply use chocolate cake mix and chocolate pudding mix.

Yield: 10-12 servings

COOKIES AND OTHER SWEET TREATS

ELLERY'S KEY LIME COOKIES

by Ellery Adams

These cookies are perfect for when you want something light and a little fruity. The combination of white chocolate chips and the key lime is delightfully refreshing. Millay, the sharp-tongued bartender from the ***Books By the Bay Mysteries,*** loves these cookies. She says they remind her of summer and that she tends to eat so much of the dough that she hardly ever bakes more than a dozen finished cookies.

INGREDIENTS
½ cup unsalted butter
1 cup granulated sugar
1 egg
1 egg yolk
2 cups all-purpose flour
1 teaspoon baking powder
½ teaspoon salt
¼ cup key lime juice (found in the baking aisle)
1 tablespoon finely grated lime zest
1 12-ounce bag white chocolate chips
½ cup confectioners' sugar

Grease the cookie sheets (or use parchment paper). In a large bowl, cream the butter, sugar, and eggs until smooth. Stir in the lime juice and lime zest. In another bowl, combine the flour, baking powder, and salt. Blend into the butter mixture. Add the white chocolate chips. (The dough will be sticky.) Refrigerate for about four hours. Form the dough into rounded teaspoons (or use a cookie scoop) and arrange on a cookie sheet. Bake 10 to 12 minutes or until lightly browned. Sift confectioners' sugar over the cookies while they're still warm.

Yield: 3 dozen cookies

CREAM CHEESE BROWNIES
by Mary Jane Maffini/Victoria Abbott

If you make these tasty treats, take care that Uncle Kev from the **Book Collector Mysteries** doesn't get wind of it. He'd make short work of them and then you would be very, very sad.

BATTER:
3 tablespoons butter
4 squares bittersweet chocolate
2 eggs (room temperature)
¾ cup sugar
1 teaspoon vanilla
½ cup flour
½ teaspoon baking powder
¼ teaspoon salt

SWIRL:
4 ounces cream cheese (no substitutions)
2 tablespoon butter, softened
1 teaspoon vanilla
¼ cup sugar
1 egg

Preheat oven to 350°. For the batter, in a microwave, melt the butter and chocolate at medium power for two minutes. In a large bowl, beat the eggs until foamy. Add ¾ cup sugar and vanilla, beat. Add butter and chocolate mixture. Combine flour, baking powder salt; add to egg-chocolate mixture stirring to combine. Pour half of the mixture into a greased 8 x 8-pan. For the swirl, cream together the cream cheese, butter, vanilla, sugar, and egg. Pour the creamed mixture over the batter in the pan in dollops. Pour the remaining chocolate batter over all. Use a knife to create a swirling effect. Bake for 30-35 minutes. Cool. Ice with chocolate cream cheese icing if desired.

CREAM CHEESE ICING:
1 square semi-sweet chocolate
¼ package of cream cheese
Confectioners' sugar
milk

Melt the chocolate in a microwave on medium for 1 minute. Cream the melted chocolate and cream cheese. Add enough Confectioners' sugar to thicken, then a tablespoon of milk or so to soften to spreading consistency. Fight off competition to eat them. Uncle Kev might have co-conspirators.

Yield: 8 brownies

AUNT HELEN'S GINGERSNAPS

by Maggie Sefton

This is my family's favorite holiday cookie. They're meant to be soft and chewy, not crispy. I've loved gingersnap cookies since I was a child and always made a batch every holiday season. Once I had a family of my own, I tried a new gingersnap recipe every year, searching for "the perfect one." Finally, I gave up searching and started tinkering with some of my old favorites and added my own special touch: grated lemon peel. Lots of it. I hope you like them as much as we do. Enjoy!

INGREDIENTS
2½ cups all-purpose flour
1 tablespoon plus 2 teaspoons ground ginger
2 teaspoons ground cinnamon
2 teaspoons baking soda
½ teaspoon salt
1½ sticks (3/4 cup) unsalted butter, softened
1 cup firmly packed dark brown sugar
1 large egg, room temperature
¼ cup unsulphured molasses
2 tablespoons freshly grated lemon peel
¼ to ½ cup granulated sugar

Preheat the oven to 350°. Lightly grease cookie sheets. Mix flour, ginger, cinnamon, baking soda, and salt in a small mixing bowl. Cream butter and brown sugar together in a medium bowl, mixing well for at least two minutes until well-blended, pale and fluffy, scraping the bowl with a rubber spatula. Beat in the egg, then the molasses and lemon peel until blended. Slowly add half the flour mixture, mixing with a wooden spoon just until blended, then add the remaining flour, mixing well.

Cover the bowl with plastic wrap and chill for 15 minutes. Roll the rounded tablespoons of dough into approximately 1¼ inch balls. Roll the balls in the granulated sugar and place 2 inches apart on a prepared cookie sheets(s). Bake just until puffed and cookies look dry—anywhere from 9 to 14 minutes, depending on your oven. (Do not overbake or the cookies will become hard). Carefully remove the cookies with a metal spatula to a wire rack to cool.

I usually double this recipe when I make it, because those amounts are easier to work with. But—be prepared to make a lot of cookies. (Note: At Colorado altitude of 5000 feet, I set my oven at 325°. Adjust your oven accordingly).

Yield: approximately 32 cookies

BROWN SUGAR-WALNUT COOKIES
by Lorraine Bartlett/ LL Bartlett

Katie Bonner, of the **Victoria Square Mysteries,** loves to bake. She finds it relaxing and fun. But she can't possibly eat everything she makes, and that's why the vendors at Artisans Alley are always happy to see her stagger under the weight of a heavy platter of cookies. These always please, they don't have a lot of ingredients, and they're always delicious.

INGREDIENTS
1 egg
1 teaspoon vanilla extract
1 cup brown sugar, firmly packed
½ cup all-purpose flour (unsifted)
¼ teaspoon baking soda
¼ teaspoon salt
1½ cups chopped walnuts

Preheat the oven to 350°. Beat the egg until fluffy. Add the sugar and vanilla and stir until smooth. Quickly stir in the flour, soda, and salt. Fold in the walnuts. Drop by the teaspoon onto a foil-lined baking sheet. Bake for 7 to 9 minutes.

Yield: 4 dozen cookies.

MRS. JONES' MOLASSES COOKIES

by Leann Sweeney

Christmas time is special on Main Street in Mercy, South Carolina, where the **Cats in Trouble Mysteries** are set. The forest green awnings of all the storefronts are all lit with tiny white lights and the shops are decorated with hand paintings on the glass windows. Belle Lowry, the owner of Belle's Beans always has plenty of these cookies available for her customers since they go so well with either coffee, tea or hot chocolate. A very old recipe from two generations ago, these were created by Belle's aunt, Margaret Jones. The cookies are absolutely "demanded" at Christmas inside Belle's Beans.

INGREDIENTS
1 cup shortening (not butter, or cookies will fall apart)
2 eggs
1 cup granulated sugar
1 cup molasses
1 teaspoon salt
1 teaspoon ginger
1 teaspoon cinnamon
½ teaspoon cream of tartar
2 teaspoons baking soda
5½-6 cups all-purpose flour

Preheat the oven to 375° Mix the ingredients in the order given. Make sure the dough is a little sticky but when pressed together, doesn't fall apart. If it does, add a little more flour. These cookies are very dependent on the humidity where you live, so you may have to play with the recipe.

Divide the dough into two or three sections; wrap

each section in waxed paper (best, though plastic wrap will work) and chill for at least 2 hours, but better overnight. Cover the cutting board or counter with a dusting of flour and roll out the dough to about ½ inch in thickness. Cut with cookie cutter. (We use a biscuit cutter—round with scalloped edges.)

Bake 8 to 10 minutes. Do Not Overbake! Cool on wire baking racks and then frost with a confectioners' sugar vanilla frosting. Let them sit until the frosting hardens and then store in sealed containers. If you leave them out, they will harden like gingersnaps.

Yield: 3 dozen cookies

CHERRY COCONUT MACAROON COOKIES

by Maggie Sefton

These are colorful and tasty cookie treats that are chewy and filled with coconut. With their bright red and green chopped cherries, they're a natural for the holiday season. But don't deny yourself a delicious treat. They're really perfect for any time of the year. Enjoy!

INGREDIENTS

1 bag (7 ounces) sweetened flaked coconut, coarsely chopped
½ cup canned almond filling
½ cup red glace cherries, chopped
½ cup green glace cherries, chopped
¼ cup granulated sugar
¼ cup all-purpose flour
¼ teaspoon salt
2 egg whites, lightly beaten

Preheat the oven to 325°. Line a large baking sheet with parchment paper or brown paper (grocery store bags will do). Add coconut, almond, cherries, sugar, flour, salt, and egg whites to a bowl and mix well. Drop the mixture by level tablespoonfuls onto a prepared baking sheet; shape into balls. Bake for 25 minutes until lightly browned but still soft in the center. Remove to wire racks to cool.

Yield: 2 dozen cookies

APPLE GINGERSNAP CRUNCH

by Hannah Reed (aka Deb Baker)

Story Fischer's grandmother is a top-notch baker. She made this for one of her Sunday family dinners, and it was a big hit. Even Story's cranky mom had to admit it was a winner. (This recipe also appears in *Buzz Off,* from the first **Queen Bee Mystery**, courtesy of Heidi Cox.)

INGREDIENTS
1 cup gingersnap cookies, crumbled
½ cup sugar
½ cup all-purpose flour
½ teaspoon salt
½ cup butter
4 apples, cut into chunks
½ cup honey
½ teaspoon cinnamon
¼ cup pecans, chopped

Preheat the oven to 350°. Mix the cookie crumbs, sugar, flour, and salt. Cut in the butter until the mixture is crumbly but holds together when pressed. Spread half over the bottom of an 8 x 8-inch baking dish and pack down lightly.

Mix together the apples, honey, and cinnamon. Spread in the pan. Add the pecans to the remaining cookie mix and spread over the top. Bake 50-60 minutes or until fruit is tender and topping is well browned.

Serve with frozen custard or ice cream.

Yield: 4-6 servings

GLAZED PECANS

by Mary Kennedy

When Taylor and Ali Blake started serving "light lunches" in the **Dream Club Mysteries,** spinach salad with glazed pecans was a big hit. They decided to make glazed pecans and sell them in pretty glass jars as a gift item.

INGREDIENTS
2 teaspoons butter
2 tablespoons brown sugar
2 teaspoons light corn syrup
pinch of salt
1 cup pecans

Melt the butter in a skillet, add the brown sugar and corn syrup; stir until combined. Add the pecans and cook, stirring constantly for five minutes. Make sure all the pecan pieces are covered with syrup. Spread on a baking tray covered with parchment paper and cool. You might want to double the recipe; these are delicious and will go fast!

Yield: 6 servings

BLOOMERS OAT SCONES
by Kate Collins

The ***Flowershop Mysteries'*** Grace Bingham, Abby Knight's British assistant who runs the coffee-and-tea parlor in the shop, shares one of her scone recipes, which are always served in the coffee-and-tea parlor side of Abby's flower shop, Bloomers. Says Grace, "Having a scone spread with clotted cream or jam and a cup of tea is a lovely way to start the day. Scones can be made with a variety of dried or fresh fruit such as currants, raisins, blueberries, or chopped nuts like pecans. I will share a very traditional yet simple recipe with you and let you decide what to put in it."

INGREDIENTS
1 large egg
6 tablespoons cold butter cut into bits
⅓ cup milk or half and half cream
1½ cup flour
1¼ cup quick oats, uncooked
2½ tablespoon granulated sugar
1 tablespoon baking powder
½ teaspoon salt (preferably sea salt)
½ cup raisins or other dried fruit, or nuts

Preheat the oven to 425°. In a small bowl, whisk the milk and egg together and set aside. Combine the dry ingredients in a separate bowl. Add the butter, and mix with your fingers until crumbling, not smooth. Add the milk mixture and stir until evenly moist. Add the dried fruit until distributed throughout. On a lightly floured surface, shape the dough into an 8-inch circle. Cut and separate into pie-shaped wedges (8-10). Bake on a greased baking sheet 12 to 15 minutes or until golden on top. Serve warm with jam, honey, or Devonshire cream. (Best eaten the day they are made.)

Yield: 8-10 servings

ZINGY GINGER SCONES

by Lorraine Bartlett/ LL Bartlett

Katie Bonner, of the **Victoria Square Mysteries,** grew up in a home where afternoon tea often supplanted dinner. While her great Aunt Lizzie often made plain scones, Katie liked to experiment. Different dried fruits—and roots—make for a different scone. If you're a fan of ginger (and isn't crystallized ginger yummy?) you'll love these tasty scones.

INGREDIENTS

2 cups biscuit baking mix
2 tablespoons sugar
1 teaspoon ground cinnamon
½ teaspoon ground ginger
¼ teaspoon ground nutmeg
⅔ cups light or heavy cream
½ cup golden raisins
2 tablespoons of candied or crystallized ginger, chopped

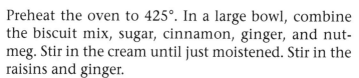

Preheat the oven to 425°. In a large bowl, combine the biscuit mix, sugar, cinnamon, ginger, and nutmeg. Stir in the cream until just moistened. Stir in the raisins and ginger.

Turn onto a floured surface; knead 10 times. Transfer the dough to a prepared baking sheet. Pat into a 9-inch circle. Cut into 8 wedges, but do not separate. Brush the tops lightly with the additional cream and sprinkle with the additional sugar. Bake for 10 to 15 minutes, or until golden brown. Cool on a wire rack for at least 10 minutes before cutting. Best served warm with butter or clotted cream.

Yield: 8 scones

ELLERY'S APPLE MAPLE GINGER CRUMBLE
by Ellery Adams

The apple trees growing in the orchards of Havenwood, Georgia, are the inspiration for this pie. After picking Gala, Red Delicious, and Granny Smith apples, Ella Mae takes her bounty back to the kitchen of the Charmed Pie Shoppe and bakes this amazing apple crumble. It's quickly become a favorite of her customers. The juicy apples combined with the zest of ginger and the sweetness of the crumble is pure magic!

INGREDIENTS
1 piecrust (homemade or store bought)
6 cups of peeled and chopped apples (pick your favorites or replace the apples with Bartlett pears)
1½ tablespoons of cornstarch
½ teaspoon of salt
¼ cup of packed brown sugar
¼ cup of pure Grade A maple syrup
1 tablespoon of lemon juice
1 teaspoon of lemon zest
½ teaspoon of ground ginger

CRUMBLE TOPPING
⅔ cup flour
½ cups old-fashioned oats
½ cup packed dark brown sugar
⅓ cup cold butter, cut into small pieces

Preheat the oven to 400°. Roll out the pie dough and place in a 9½-inch deep-dish pie pan. Put in the freezer to set. Place the chopped apples in a large bowl with the cornstarch, ginger, brown sugar, maple syrup, lemon juice, and lemon zest. Toss well using your fingers. Place the apple mixture into the pie dish. Place the pie into the center oven rack and bake for 45 minutes. While baking, take all the crumble topping ingredients and place them in a bowl. Use your hands and mix the ingredients until large crumbs form. Refrigerate until use. After the 45 minutes are up, remove the pie and reduce the heat to 375°. Sprinkle the crumb topping evenly over the pie and bake for another 15 minutes. Cool on a wire rack for at least one hour. Serve with a scoop of vanilla ice cream.

Yield: 6-8 servings

BELLE'S BLUEBERRY MUFFINS

by Leann Sweeney

Belle Lowry, owner of Belle's Beans (the coffee shop on Main Street in the *Cats in Trouble Mysteries*) likes to plan ahead. Since she always brings homemade baked goods to the shop, she makes this muffin batter and stores it in the fridge in a sealed container. It will keep for 2-3 weeks and she has a fresh batch of muffins for her customers several mornings in a row. No one can pass on these muffins and Jillian Hart, the main character in the series, always feels lucky if she arrives early enough to nab a muffin to go with her morning coffee.

INGREDIENTS

⅔ cup shortening

1 cup granulated sugar

3 eggs

3 cups plus 2 heaping teaspoons all-purpose flour

2 heaping teaspoons of baking powder

1 teaspoon salt

1 cup milk

1 tall can well-drained blueberries or one pint of
    fresh blueberries

Preheat the oven to 375°. Cream together the shortening and sugar until fluffy. Add the eggs one at a time and mix well with an electric mixer. Alternately mix in the dry ingredients and milk until well combined, but do not overbeat. Fold in the blueberries. Bake in a muffin pan with paper liners, for about 25 minutes. Store the remaining the batter in the fridge for 2-3 weeks—or if you have a crowd, use it all at once.

Yield: 3 dozen muffins

ELLERY'S RASPBERRY TRUFFLE FUDGE
by Ellery Adams

Let's face it: every now and then a girl needs a hit of chocolate. Something smooth and rich and sweet. Something to make her feel like a kid again. For Olivia Limoges of the **Books By the Bay Mysteries,** a bite of this fudge can take her back to her childhood. To long walks on the beach scavenging for seashells, to hanging sand dollars and starfish on the Christmas tree, to the sight of her mother in the kitchen stirring fudge in the ceramic mixing bowl with the chip in its rim, humming in pleasure as her wooden spoon moved through the melted chocolate. Now it's your turn. Mix up a batch of this fudge and prepare to feel spoiled!

INGREDIENTS
3 cups semi-sweet chocolate chips
1 14-ounce can sweetened condensed milk
1½ teaspoons vanilla extract
¼ cup heavy whipping cream
¼ cup Chambord liqueur
2 cups white chocolate chips
cooking spray

Spray an 8 x 8-inch pan (for thicker fudge) or a 9 x 9-inch pan with non-stick cooking spray and line with wax paper. In a microwave-safe bowl, combine 3 cups chocolate chips and sweetened condensed milk. Heat in the microwave until the chocolate melts, stirring occasionally. Be careful not to overcook. Stir in the vanilla. Spread into the pan, and cool to room temperature. In a microwave-safe bowl, combine the cream, liqueur, and 2 cups white chocolate chips.

Heat in the microwave until the chocolate melts; stir until smooth. Cool to lukewarm, then pour over the fudge layer. Refrigerate until both layers are completely set, 1-1½ hours. Cut into 1-inch squares.

Yield: 64-81 pieces

MAGGIE'S CHOCOLATE MINT FUDGE
by Maggie Sefton

Chocolate fudge has been a favorite of mine ever since I was a child. I've seen various recipes posted over the years in newsletters, magazines, cooking shows—everywhere there are chocolate lovers. As a young mother years ago, I wanted to put my own stamp on my favorite chocolate treat. Since I loved the flavor of mint and chocolate together, I decided to substitute peppermint flavoring for vanilla. Family and friends have loved it ever since. And it's always the highlight of my Christmas holiday gift boxes. Enjoy!

INGREDIENTS
1 medium-to-large jar of marshmallow cream
1 12-ounce can evaporated milk
1 stick (½ cup) of salted butter (no substitutions)
3 cups granulated sugar
1 teaspoon salt
2 12-ounce packages of semi-sweet chocolate chips/morsels
1 tablespoon peppermint flavoring

A large thick-bottomed pot is recommended in order to keep the fudge from overcooking. Before starting, line 2 8 x 8-inch pans with aluminum foil. Grease lightly with butter (do not use oil or margarine).

Place the marshmallow cream in a pot over medium heat, then stir in the evaporated milk, stirring slowly. Cut the stick of butter into 8 pieces and drop into the simmering mixture. Stir in the salt. Adjust the heat to medium-high and add the sugar one-half cup at a time, stirring well after each addition.

Continue stirring as the sugar mixture starts to bubble. Stirring constantly, cook for five minutes, no more. (I cannot emphasize this enough.)

Remove from the heat and immediately stir in the packages of semi-sweet chocolate chips/morsels, one package at a time, stirring vigorously. Add the peppermint flavoring, stirring well until blended. Pour the fudge into the two pans. Let cool on the counter for several minutes, then place the pans in the fridge to set up and cool completely. Cut into 1-inch pieces. Super rich and delicious. Enjoy!

Yield: 128 pieces

PEANUT BUTTER OATMEAL BARS
by Lorraine Bartlett/ LL Bartlett

Katie Bonner, of the **Victoria Square Mysteries,** has such a huge sweet tooth, that even her dentist is worried about it. But that doesn't stop her from baking a couple of times a week—and sharing the bounty with her friends and vendors at Artisans Alley. Her great Aunt Lizzie was a Scot who believed you could add oatmeal to just about everything. It sure proved true with these cookies.

INGREDIENTS
½ cup butter, softened
½ cup sugar
½ cup brown sugar, firmly packed
½ cup peanut butter, crunchy or smooth
1 egg, beaten
1 teaspoon vanilla extract
1 cup all-purpose flour
½ cup quick-cooking oats
1 teaspoon baking soda
¼ teaspoon salt
1 cup (6 ounces) milk chocolate chips

ICING
½ cup confectioners' sugar
2 tablespoons creamy peanut butter
2 tablespoons milk

Preheat the oven to 350°. In a mixing bowl, cream the butter, sugars, and peanut butter. Add the egg and vanilla; mix well. In another bowl, combine the flour, oats, baking soda, and salt. Stir into the creamed mixture. Spread into a greased 13 x 9-inch baking pan.

Sprinkle with chocolate chips. Bake for 20 to 25 minutes or until lightly browned. Cool for 10 minutes. Combine the icing ingredients; drizzle over the bars.

Yield: 3-4 dozen bars

MAGGIE'S CINNAMON ROLLS
by Maggie Sefton

When I submitted the very first novel in the **Kelly Flynn Knitting Mystery series,** *Knit One, Kill Two,* my editor requested a recipe for the yummy cinnamon rolls Kelly enjoys in the first chapter. I was expecting a request for one of the scarves mentioned in the book, but a recipe? Since these over-sized cinnamon rolls were a local favorite in several Fort Collins, Colorado, cafés, I thought I'd ask one of the local chefs for his/her recipe. To my surprise, every one of the chefs/cooks/owners refused, claiming: "old family recipe." Huh? I thought. Didn't they realize it was free advertising? Oh, well. Since they refused to cooperate, I simply returned to my recipe files and combined one of my old recipes with one from my 93-year old aunt Ann in Virginia. And—I have to be honest— these cinnamon rolls are way better than the ones in the cafés! These are more tender, the filling has more brown sugar and spices, and the lemon cream cheese icing is much richer, too. A super yummy treat for any time of year. Enjoy!

DOUGH:
3½-4 cups all-purpose flour
1 package active dry yeast
1 cup whole milk
⅓ cup butter
⅓ cup granulated sugar
½ teaspoon salt
1 beaten egg

FILLING:
2 tablespoons melted butter

1 cup dark brown sugar, firmly packed
3 teaspoons ground cinnamon

LEMON CREAM CHEESE FROSTING:
4 ounces cream cheese, softened
2 tablespoons butter, softened
1 tablespoon lemon juice
2 cups confectioners' sugar

Optional: ½ cup walnuts, pecans, or raisins

Stir together the yeast and 1½ cups of flour in a large mixing bowl and set aside. In a saucepan over medium-low heat, combine the milk, butter, and sugar. Add the salt and heat until warm and the butter is melted. Slowly add the beaten egg to the flour mixture, stirring until well-blended. Beat with an electric mixer 3 minutes, stirring in as much of the remaining flour as possible. Place the dough on a lightly-floured surface and knead until smooth and elastic (about 5 minutes). Shape the dough into a ball and place in a lightly-greased bowl, turning once. Then cover and let rise in a warm place until doubled (about 1-½ hours).

To make the frosting: Combine the softened cream cheese and butter. Stir until light and fluffy. Add the lemon juice. Beat in the confectioner's sugar gradually until well-blended and smooth. If needed, add the half and half until you get the desired consistency. Set aside.

Punch down the dough and turn onto a lightly-floured surface. Cover and let rest for 10 minutes. Grease a cookie sheet or large baking pan(s) and set aside. Roll the dough into a 10 x 18-inch rectangle. Spread with the melted butter. Stir together the brown sugar and cinnamon and sprinkle over the dough.

Add the nuts or raisins if desired. Tightly roll up the dough from the long side. Pinch and seal the ends. Cut the dough into one-inch sections and place on a prepared baking sheet or pan. Cover and let rise until double (40-60 minutes). Brush the rolls with melted butter. Bake in a 350° oven for 25 to 30 minutes * until golden brown. Remove rolls to a wire rack and frost while still warm.

• Warning: This yeast sweet dough recipe is very sensitive to heat. Try a lower oven temperature the first time. Since I live in Colorado at a higher altitude, I set my oven for 325° and bake the rolls for 23 minutes. For best results, please adjust the baking time and temperature accordingly.

Yield: approximately 12 rolls

BELLE'S SWITCHEROO BLONDE BROWNIES
by Leann Sweeney

In the **Cats in Trouble Mysteries**, Belle Lowry owns local coffee spot Belle's Beans right in the center of picturesque Mercy, South Carolina, and just a stone's throw from Jillian Hart's favorite stop in town, The Cotton Company. This shop is floor-to-ceiling quilting fabric and after hours looking for just the right bolts of quilting fabric for her kitty quilts, Jillian always heads straight to Belle's Beans afterward. Belle not only serves the best coffee in the South, she likes to have a variety of goodies to go along with a latte or a cappuccino. Belle makes everything from scratch herself and for this treat, she uses her basic blonde brownie recipe but varies the combination of flavored baking chips she adds to the brownies. Jillian likes the peanut butter-chocolate the best!

INGREDIENTS
¾ cup brown sugar, firmly packed
¾ cup granulated sugar
1 cup butter, softened
2 eggs
½ teaspoon vanilla
2¼ cups all-purpose flour
1 teaspoon baking soda
½ teaspoon salt
1½ cups peanut butter chips
1 cup chocolate chips
OR 1½ cups vanilla chips
1 cup cinnamon chips
OR 1½ cup chocolate chips
1 cup caramel chips

Preheat the oven to 350°. Cream the first 5 ingredients until fluffy. Add in the dry ingredients, except for the chips, and combine well. Fold in whatever combination of chips you want. Feel free to experiment with your own combinations. Spread in a lightly greased 13 x 9-inch pan. Bake for 25 to 30 min.

Yield: 20 brownies

CHOCOLATE PECAN RUM BALLS
by Maggie Sefton

I've always loved any combination of chocolate, nuts, and rum. So, it wasn't hard for me to tinker with one of my recipes until I could combine all three tastes. Again, this is a holiday favorite of my family, and I've been making it for years as part of my holiday goodies gift boxes, which I send out in early December.

INGREDIENTS
2 cups crushed vanilla wafers
2 cups confectioners' sugar
3 cups chopped pecans
4 tablespoons cocoa
4 tablespoons light corn syrup
½ cup dark rum
½ cup superfine granulated sugar

Combine the crushed wafers and confectioners' sugar, then add the chopped pecans and cocoa. Mix well. Add the corn syrup, then rum, and mix well. Shape into 1-inch balls. Roll in the granulated sugar. Place each ball in a covered container and store in refrigerator until ready to serve—or mail as presents. (Storing in an airtight container allows the flavors to become stronger and even more delicious). Enjoy!

Yield: approximately 4 dozen

APPLE FRITTERS

by Lorraine Bartlett/ LL Bartlett

Artisans Alley (on Victoria Square) is located in the core of apple country along the Lake Ontario shore, where scores of apple varieties grow. Can there be anything more comforting than an apple fritter (or a LOT of them) for breakfast, lunch, dinner—or just a snack? Why not try this recipe and find out?

INGREDIENTS
1 cup cake flour (sifted)
¾ teaspoon baking powder
¼ teaspoon salt
1 egg
⅓ cup milk
¾ cup chopped peeled tart apple
4 teaspoons butter, melted
1 tablespoon granulated sugar
1 tablespoon orange juice
¼ teaspoon vanilla extract
oil for frying
confectioners' sugar

In a bowl, combine the flour, baking power, and salt. In another bowl, beat the egg and milk. Add the apple, butter, sugar, orange juice, and vanilla; mix well. Stir into the dry ingredients until just moistened.

In an electric skillet or deep fryer, heat ¼ inch of oil to 375°. Drop the batter by rounded tablespoons into the oil. Fry until golden brown on both sides. Drain on paper towels. Dust with the confectioners' sugar. Serve warm.

Yield: 2-3 servings

QUICK AS A FLASH PEACH CRISP

by Mary Kennedy

Ali Blake says that any fruit will be delicious in this crisp, but since The **Dream Club Mysteries** are set in Savannah, she decided to use Georgia peaches. You can use fresh fruit or frozen.

INGREDIENTS
4 cups sliced peaches, fresh or frozen
½ teaspoon cinnamon
1 cup brown sugar
¾ cup old fashioned oats
¾ cup all-purpose flour
1 stick butter (½ cup), softened

Preheat the oven to 350°. Arrange the peaches in bottom of a greased 8 x 8-inch baking pan. Mix cinnamon, brown sugar, oats, and flour. Cut in the softened butter until the mixture resembles coarse crumbs. Spread over the peaches. Bake until golden brown, approximately 40 minutes.

Yield: 6 servings

KITTY'S FRIED DOUGHNUTS
by Deb Baker (aka Hannah Reed)

Finns and Swedes love their bakeries. A cup of strong coffee and a doughnut will make them happy all day long. Gertie Johnson's friend, Kitty, has been known to carry these around in her purse in case she gets hungry later. The secret to perfect doughnuts is the mashed potatoes. Don't forget to dunk them in coffee. (This recipe was also included in *Murder Passes the Buck, **a Gertie Johnson Backwoods Mystery.***)

INGREDIENTS
5 cups white flour
4 teaspoons baking powder
1 teaspoon baking soda
1½ teaspoons salt
½ teaspoon cinnamon
1 cup mashed potatoes
1½ cups sugar
2 eggs
¼ cup melted butter
1 cup buttermilk
1 teaspoon vanilla
½ teaspoon grated lemon rind
oil for frying
confectioners' sugar or granulated sugar
cinnamon (optional)

Sift together the flour, baking powder, baking soda, salt, and cinnamon. Add the mashed potatoes and sugar. Mix well. Blend in the eggs and melted butter. In a separate bowl, combine the buttermilk, vanilla, and lemon rind. Add to the flour mix, blend well, cover, and let stand for 15 minutes.

Roll out the dough and cut with a doughnut cutter. Fry in oil in a pan or deep fryer until golden brown. Turn with a fork, then brown the other side. Remove and lay on paper towel to drain and cool. Shake the doughnuts in a bag with granulated or confectioners' sugar. Try ½ cup confectioners' sugar and 1 teaspoon cinnamon for a special treat. Serve warm.

Yield: 18 doughnuts

MAGGIE'S FLAN

by Maggie Sefton

Flan is a yummy rich custard that I've loved since the first time I tasted it. However, I noticed that some cooks had the knack of caramelizing sugar just enough so that the burned flavor didn't intrude too much, and other cooks did not. The almost-burned flavor would often spoil my enjoyment of the rich dessert, so I set out to find or develop a recipe that could avoid that problem—and I did! In fact, this recipe avoids "burnout" entirely by using brown sugar instead. Once again, I tinkered around with other ingredients until I made it my own. Personally, I think the dark brown sugar I use makes an even richer sauce that cooks in the bottom of the pan and is later spooned across the flan. This custard cooks in the classic "Bain Marie" water bath in the oven.

INGREDIENTS
8 eggs
⅔ cup granulated sugar
¼ teaspoon salt
2 12-ounce cans evaporated milk
2 teaspoons vanilla extract
½ cup dark brown sugar, firmly packed

Preheat the oven to 350°. Boil the water in a kettle, then keep on a simmer. Beat the eggs until the yolks and whites are well-blended. Add the sugar and salt and mix well. Beat in the evaporated milk and add the vanilla. Mix well. Crumble the brown sugar onto the bottom of a bread loaf pan and gently pour the custard into the pan over the brown sugar. Place the loaf pan inside a shallow pan containing hot but not boiling water. Bake for 1 hour or until a knife inserted in the center comes out clean. Remove from the oven; cool on a rack, and refrigerate overnight. Before serving, run a knife around the edges of pan to loosen the flan, then turn out onto a small platter. Scrape all the melted brown sugar syrup from the pan onto flan. Serve with the melted sauce.

Yield: 12 servings

ELLERY'S NO CRUST CRANBERRY PECAN TART

by Ellery Adams

This is a cake-like tart that is simple to make and easy to carry to a friend's house as a hostess gift or to add to the holiday dessert table. The tartness of the cranberries and the crunchy pecans provide an explosion of tastes and textures, while the two extracts bring out the sweet, cinnamon flavors of the dough. This is a great dessert to make with children as it's nearly impossible to mess up!

INGREDIENTS
1 cup all-purpose flour
1 cup granulated sugar
2 cups fresh cranberries
½ cup chopped pecans
½ cup butter, melted
2 eggs
¼ teaspoon pure almond extract
¾ teaspoon vanilla extract
½ teaspoon cinnamon
¼ teaspoon ground cloves

Preheat the oven to 350°. Grease one 9-inch pie pan. Combine the flour, sugar, and salt. Stir in the cranberries and the pecans, and toss to coat. Stir in the butter, beaten eggs, vanilla and almond extracts. Add cinnamon and cloves. Spread the batter into the prepared pan. It will look more like cake batter than pie filling.

Bake for 40 to 45 minutes, or until a wooden pick inserted near the center comes out clean. Serve warm. A scoop of vanilla ice cream or real whipped cream tastes great on this pie.

Yield: 6-8 servings

RHUBARB MERINGUE TORTE
by Hannah Reed/Deb Baker

Rhubarb is plentiful in Wisconsin during the spring months. It's the first sign that spring has sprung. Story Fischer's honeybees are starting to forage. A buzz is in the air. Gather an armful of rhubarb and make the best torte ever. (This recipe also appears in *Mind Your Own Beeswax*, third in the **Queen Bee Mysteries**, courtesy of Martha Gatchel.)

4 cups chopped rhubarb

THE CRUST:
2 cups all-purpose flour
2 tablespoons granulated sugar
¼ teaspoon salt
1 cup butter

Preheat the oven to 350°. Mix all the ingredients together and press into the bottom of 13 x 9-inch pan. Bake for 20 minutes. Cool. Add the rhubarb.

THE CUSTARD:
4 egg yolks
¾ cup milk
1 cup honey
2 tablespoons all-purpose flour

Whisk together the above ingredients and cook in a saucepan over medium heat until bubbly. Pour the custard over the crust and rhubarb. Bake for 20 min.

MERINGUE:
4 egg whites

1 cup granulated sugar

Beat the egg whites with an electric mixer on high; add the sugar 1 tablespoon at a time until stiff peaks occur. Top the custard mix with the meringue. Bake for 10 minutes. Allow the tart to cool for one hour.

Yield: 8-10 servings

CHOCOLATE SIN

by Lorraine Bartlett/ LL Bartlett

Brenda Stanley, one of the three main characters in my *Jeff Resnick Mystery series,* is a chocoholic. It doesn't take much to become one. She says she makes these truffles for her husband, physician Richard Alpert, but she really makes them for herself. (And why not?) These candies truly are sinful, and sinfully simple to make.

INGREDIENTS

2 cups (12 ounces) milk chocolate chips
1 tablespoon shortening
½ cup raisins
½ cup peanuts (or use your favorite nut: almonds, walnuts, you can even toss in a half cup of mini marshmallows)

In a microwave-safe bowl, melt the chocolate in the microwave for 2-3 minutes, stirring every 30 seconds. Stir in the rest of the ingredients. Drop by tablespoons onto waxed paper. Chill until ready to serve.

Yield: 12 servings

ENGLISH TOFFEE CANDY
by Mary Kennedy

Dr. Maggie Walsh keeps a tin of these on her desk at WYME Radio for her guests, but the crew always gobbles them up. Vera Mae Atkins, her producer, says a box of this candy is the perfect hostess gift.

INGREDIENTS
40 saltines
2 sticks (1 cup) butter
1 cup packed brown sugar
2 cups semi-sweet chocolate chips
1 cup chopped nuts (any kind)

Pre-heat oven to 400°. Place a sheet of foil or parchment paper on a large cookie sheet. Spray the foil with non-stick cooking spray. Arrange the saltines in a single layer on a greased or foil-lined cookie sheet so they touch. In small saucepan, mix the butter and sugar. Stir constantly and bring to a rolling boil. Boil for 3 minutes. Pour the butter-sugar mixture over the crackers. Bake for 5 minutes and cool for one minute. Sprinkle with the chocolate chips. The chocolate will soften immediately. Take a spatula and spread the softened chocolate over the saltines. While still warm, gently press the nuts into the chocolate. Refrigerate for at least one hour before breaking apart.

Yield: 8 servings

EASY TOFFEE BARS

by Maggie Sefton

This toffee bar candy recipe is as easy to make as it looks. Great for holiday gift-giving, cookie exchanges, or any occasion where people love tasty treats. It also ships well and keeps quite a while in the fridge. Enjoy!

INGREDIENTS
4½ cups quick cooking oats
1 cup dark brown sugar, firmly packed
¾ cup butter, melted
½ cup dark corn syrup
1 tablespoon vanilla
½ teaspoon salt
1 12-ounce package semi-sweet chocolate chips
2 tablespoons butter
⅔ cup chopped pecans

Preheat the oven to 450°. Grease 15 x 10-inch pan. (You can use a 13 x 9-inch pan.) Combine the oats, sugar, butter, corn syrup, vanilla, and salt. Mix well. Firmly press the mixture into the pan. Bake 12 minutes or until mixture is brown and bubbly. Remove to a wire rack until completely cool. In saucepan over low heat, melt the chocolate and butter, stirring constantly until smooth. Spread evenly over the oat base; sprinkle with nuts. Chill until set then cut into bars or squares. (You may also melt the chocolate and butter in a glass dish in the microwave on high for 1 to 2 minutes, stirring often until smooth).

Yield: 36 pieces

THE PERFECT SWEET AND SALTY SNACK
by Mary Kennedy

Lola Walsh, from the **Talk Radio Mysteries,** loves to have these on hand in case one of her showbiz friends happens to drop by. She said Martha Cheves, a gourmet cook, gave her the recipe and it's the perfect late afternoon snack.

INGREDIENTS
1 16-ounce box of cereal squares (corn, wheat, rice, or a mixture)
2 cups whole pecans (you can also use walnuts)
½ cup corn syrup
½ cup packed brown sugar
½ stick (¼ cup) butter
1 teaspoon vanilla
½ teaspoon baking powder

Preheat the oven to 250°. Combine the cereal and the pecans in a 9 x 13-inch baking dish. In a 2-cup microwavable bowl, mix the corn syrup, brown sugar, and butter. Microwave on high 90 seconds. Stir. Microwave on high for an additional minute or two until the mixture is boiling. Stir in the vanilla and baking powder. Pour the mixture over the cereal and nuts. Stir until evenly coated. Bake 1 hour, stirring every 20 minutes.

Yield: about 2 quarts

EXCITING EXTRAS

EGGS WITH ARUGULA & LEMON
by Deb Baker (aka Hannah Reed)

Arugula has such a unique flavor, and goes with everything, even eggs. Arugula grows quickly, then as soon as you blink, it bolts. So make sure you have eggs around the minute it peaks and prepare yourself for a very pleasant morning brunch.

INGREDIENTS
2 tablespoons olive oil
6 green onions, chopped (include some of the green part)
3 cloves of garlic, minced
7-9 cups of arugula
1 teaspoon kosher salt
5 eggs, stirred together in a bowl
½ lemon
black pepper

Cook the onions and garlic in olive oil until beginning to brown (about 4 minutes). Add the arugula and salt, and cook a minute or two until the arugula is wilted. Add the eggs and cook until set. Squeeze lemon juice over the top and sprinkle with pepper.

Yield: 3-4 servings

BLOOMERS EGG SKILLET
by Kate Collins

If you've read any of the **Flower Shop Mysteries,** you know that at Bloomers, Abby Knight's flower shop, Monday morning breakfast is a tradition, so what better way to start off our week than with an authentic Bloomers breakfast? Abby's assistant, Lottie Domkowski, a Kentucky gal, shares her special egg skillet recipe.

INGREDIENTS
6 large eggs
½ cup feta or goat cheese, crumbled
sea salt, pepper
olive oil
leftover veggies (optional)

Lightly coat the bottom of heavy skillet with olive oil. Heat on medium low. Break yhe eggs into a bowl and whip until well mixed. Pour the mixture into the skillet, turn the heat to low. Sprinkle in the cheese crumbles. Salt and pepper lightly. If you have any leftover veggies, such as asparagus spears, spinach, tomatoes, or cooked onion, chop them into fine pieces and toss them in. The more the merrier. As the eggs cook, lift the edges with a spatula to let the uncooked egg run underneath. When the middle is set and the bottom is starting to brown, slide onto a big plate, fold in half, cut into wedges and—down the hatch! Grab a cup of coffee or tea and enjoy!

Yield: 3 servings

DEVILED EGGS
(because life should be a picnic)

by Mary Jane Maffini

Deviled eggs seem to be making a comeback and high time, too. They're easy and almost everyone seems to love them. They disappear so fast they belong in a mystery.

INGREDIENTS

10 large eggs

¾ cup mayonnaise (or more if you like it creamier)

2 teaspoons Dijon mustard

½ teaspoon sea salt (or to taste–the Dijon brings some saltiness!)

¼ teaspoon freshly ground pepper (or to taste)

½ teaspoon paprika

⅛ teaspoon cayenne pepper (optional)

Fresh chives chopped

Place eggs a medium saucepan, and cover with cold water. Bring to a boil. Remove from heat. Cover; let stand 12 minutes. Using a slotted spoon, transfer eggs to an ice-water bath.

When eggs are cool, peel, and cut in half lengthwise. Carefully remove yolks, keeping whites intact and transferring whites and yolks to separate bowls. Refrigerate whites.

Add mayonnaise, Dijon, salt, pepper, paprika and cayenne to yolks. Mash with a fork or a potato masher until smooth. Cover, and refrigerate until stiff; about 30 minutes

Mound yolk mixture in each egg-white half. Garnish with chives.

Yield: 20 egg halves

GOOD FOR YOU GRITS

by Deb Baker (aka Hannah Reed)

My southern dad loved grits. I do, too, but I like them with lots of butter, the more the merrier. Which isn't all that good for me. So I came up with this variation. I'm not sure it's any better health wise, but ... who cares?

INGREDIENTS
2¼ cups water
¾ cup evaporated milk
¾ cup quick grits
½ teaspoon salt
pepper to taste
½ cup low-fat shredded cheddar

In a medium saucepan, bring the water and milk to a boil. Stir in the grits and add the salt and pepper. Cover and cook for 5 minutes or until thick. Remove from the heat and stir in the cheese until melted.

Yield: 4 servings

BEST EVER CORNBREAD
by Mary Kennedy

Ali and Taylor Blake quickly learned that Southerners are big fans of cornbread. When they went to Persia Walker for advice, she gave them her favorite recipe. This cornbread was so popular, everyone in the ***Dream Club Mysteries*** wanted a copy.

INGREDIENTS
2 large eggs
1 stick (½ cup) melted butter
2 cups Bisquick
½ cup cornmeal
½ cup sugar
1 cup milk

Preheat the oven to 350°. Whisk eggs and butter together and then add the remaining ingredients. Do not over mix. (Batter will be lumpy.) Turn into a greased 8 by 8-inch square pan. Bake 25 to 35 minutes.

Yield: 8 servings

ALL PURPOSE GRAVY
by Kate Collins

This gravy is delicious with any type of meat or over mashed potatoes or rice. It has become our family favorite for Thanksgiving dinner. This version makes 4 cups. To double: use a larger skillet or a Dutch oven and double the cooking time, too. Whisk constantly when adding broths. Browning the veggies and flour gives the gravy its color.

INGREDIENTS
3 tablespoons unsalted butter
1 carrot, peeled and chopped fine
1 stalk celery, chopped fine
1 onion, minced
¼ cup flour
2 cups low sodium chicken broth
2 cups low sodium beef broth
1 bay leaf
¼ teaspoon thyme
5 whole black peppercorns

Melt the butter in a large saucepan over medium-high heat. Add the veggies, cook until soft and well-browned, about 9 minutes. Stir in the flour and cook, stirring constantly, until thoroughly browned, about 5 minutes.

Gradually whisk in the broths and bring to a boil. Add the bay leaf, thyme, and peppercorns. Simmer, stirring occasionally, until thickened, 20 to 25 minutes, skimming off any foam that forms on the surface.

Pour the gravy through a fine mesh strainer (or cheesecloth) into a clean saucepan, pressing on the

solids to the extract liquid. Discard the solids, or combine them with the leftover gravy and use as a vegetable sauce over leftover potatoes or rice for another
meal. Serve with any type of meat.

• This recipe can be refrigerated in an airtight container up to 4 days, or frozen. Reheat over a low heat,
whisking to recombine, or microwave 1 to 3 minutes,
stirring until smooth.

Yield: 4 cups

NONNA'S PIZZA DOUGH
by Mary Jane Maffini

My daughter Victoria and I write the book collector mysteries as Victoria Abbott. The eccentric Italian cook, Signora Panetone, is a whiz in the kitchen. She's a bit like some Italian nonnas (grandmothers) that we've met. Although she'd never share a recipe, we are betting that her pizza crust is a lot like this traditional thick crust version served in our family.

This recipe is for my mother-in-law's deep pizza. She baked it in rectangular shaped pans and cut it into squares. It was always welcome and wonderful. There was never one square left. Now that she no longer has a kitchen, we've all tried to reconstruct it. Here's the closest we've come. No complaints, but of course, it's only 98% of the original.

By the way, this is for pizza dough that's at least an inch thick, chewy and bready with lots of cheese and nice light tomato sauce. No thin crusts around here, although we like them elsewhere.

INGREDIENTS
1 tablespoon granulated yeast (or one envelope)
1 cup warm water
1 teaspoon sugar
1 egg, beaten
¼ cup oil
3-3¼ cups all-purpose flour (or more if needed)
1½ teaspoon salt
cornmeal (optional)

In a large bowl, melt the yeast in warm water, and sprinkle in the sugar. Leave it for 10 minutes. Add the beaten egg and oil. Stir in the flour and salt. Mix until the dough is smooth and elastic and the flour is all absorbed. Let the dough rise for an hour or until double, covered (tip: heat oven to 110 degrees and turn off immediately for an almost ideal temperature). Punch down the dough and divide it in half. Roll out to 2 inches thick on a floured board. Let the dough rest for ten minutes. Roll again to 2 inches thick. Shape into and oiled baking tray, pizza tray, or jelly roll pan, dusted with cornmeal if you like. Cover and let rise again (in warm spot).

Finish off with your favorite tomato-based pizza sauce, different types of grated cheese and your preferred toppings. Cheese and bacon has been popular in our newer version as is chicken, pesto and goat cheese.

Preheat the oven to 425° and bake for 15 minutes or until done, or bake for ten minutes – then put toppings on and finish baking. You can freeze the dough, or freeze the pizzas cooked or uncooked with or without toppings. Lots of options here! Thaw and bake a few minutes longer than for fresh.

Yield: 1 large or 2 small pizzas

SOUTHERN SPOON BREAD
by Maggie Sefton

Spoon bread is not widely known outside of the southern United States. Once visitors to the region taste it, however, many of them decide they want to try it in their own homes. The rich flavors and soft texture make this cornmeal-based quick bread a perfect accompaniment to many meals. If you like cornbread, you should really enjoy southern spoon bread. Give it a try!

INGREDIENTS
3 cups milk (whole or 2%), divided
¾ cups cornmeal, yellow
1 teaspoon salt
2 tablespoons butter
2 eggs, separated
1 teaspoon baking powder

Preheat the oven to 375°. Put 2 cups milk in the top of a double boiler and heat to scalding. Meanwhile, mix the remaining milk with the cornmeal, then add to the scalded milk and cook, stirring often, for 30 minutes. Cool slightly. Whip the egg whites until stiff and set aside.

Add the butter, salt, and beaten egg yolks to the cornmeal mixture and mix well. Add the baking powder and mix. Fold in the egg whites. Carefully pour the mixture into a greased casserole and bake for about 30 minutes.

Yield: 6-8 servings

POLENTA: TRADITIONAL OR STARS

by Mary Jane Maffin/Victoria Abbott

Historically, polenta has been a beloved peasant food. In the **Book Collector Mysteries** Signora Panetone serves mountains of it with savory meat sauce and lots of freshly grated cheese. It really perks up the grand dining room of The Van Alst House. She does not make snazzy little stars out of it, although we sometimes like to and you might think it's fun, too.

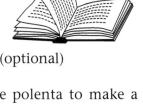

INGREDIENTS
1 cup coarse polenta
3 1/2 cups water or broth
salt and pepper to taste
1 tablespoon butter or olive oil (optional)

Mix 1 cup cold water with the polenta to make a smooth paste. Bring the remaining 2½ cups of water to a boil in a large pot. Add the polenta mixture to the boiling water in a thin stream. Boil over high heat, stirring steadily for 2–3 minutes. Add a little salt and pepper. Reduce the heat to medium-low and simmer until it thickens and pulls away from the side of the pot. Give it a stir every five minutes or so for 30–40 minutes.

Serve hot with spaghetti or mushroom sauce and freshly grated Parmesan cheese, or make stars by pouring onto a baking sheet greased with the butter or oil and smoothing it to about ¾ inch thick. Cover with plastic wrap. Chill until firm. Cut into stars or other shapes and sauté it in a little olive oil or butter. You can also grill the stars or slices. They're quite pretty with grill marks.

RHUBARB CHUTNEY
by Lorraine Bartlett/ LL Bartlett

Ever wonder what to do with all the rhubarb in your yard? If you like chutney, you'll love this recipe. I first made it when I was about twelve years old. We enjoyed it for years and then the recipe mysteriously disappeared. Well, I found it recently and I can't wait to use up the bounty of my yard with the next crop of rhubarb.

INGREDIENTS
6 cups rhubarb, chopped fine
4 cups minced onions
4 cups brown sugar, firmly packed
1 quart cider vinegar
3 teaspoons salt
1 teaspoon cinnamon
1 teaspoon ground ginger
1 teaspoon allspice
¼ teaspoon cayenne powder

In a large saucepan or Dutch oven, mix all ingredients together and cook until thick (about 1 hour), stirring from time to time. Ladle into hot sterilized jars and seal. Store in the refrigerator after opening.

Yield: 8 pints

THOUSAND ISLAND DRESSING

by Deb Baker (aka Hannah Reed)

My father-in-law made this from scratch the first time I met the family. It was love at first sight, for the family and for this delicious dressing. Making salad dressing is so easy, I wonder why we usually reach for a store-bought bottle.

INGREDIENTS:
1 cup mayonnaise
1 tablespoon sweet pickle relish
2 tablespoons chili sauce
1 tablespoon green pepper, chopped (optional)
1 teaspoon green olives stuffed with pimento
1 hard-boiled egg, chopped fine

Mix together and refrigerate until chilled. Lasts 4 to 5 days.

Yield: 4 servings

PIMENTO CHEESE SPREAD
by Mary Kennedy

What could be more southern than home-made pimento cheese spread? Pimento cheese sandwiches are
one of the most popular items on the menu in Oldies
but Goodies, the candy shop/café in the ***Dream Club
Mysteries***. Ali and Taylor Blake like this simple recipe
because it's foolproof and it makes 4 cups of cheese
spread.

INGREDIENTS
2 7-ounce jars pimentos, drained
30 ounces sharp cheddar cheese, grated
1 cup mayonnaise

Process the pimentos in a blender or food processor
until smooth. Using an electric mixer, beat the cheese
and pimentos. Beat in the mayonnaise and chill.
Southerners would serve this on white sandwich
bread, and some folks like grilled pimento cheese
sandwiches. They're delicious either way.

Yield: 10 sandwiches

MAIN STREET HOT DOG SAUCE

by Leann Sweeney

In the **Cats in Trouble Mysteries**, the Main Street Diner is a frequent hang-out for Mercy, South Carolina residents. The decor is 1950-ish with a jukebox at every wooden booth. There's also a long curving counter with red-leather cushioned stools. The menu consists of burgers, fries, milkshakes, and the best chilidogs ever. These very special hot dogs are so popular they are often ordered by the dozen for takeout, and go out wrapped in wax paper and put in brown paper sacks bearing the Main Street Diner logo. The secret is all in that hot dog sauce—and cat lover, quilter and amateur sleuth Jillian Hart managed to talk the owner into sharing the recipe for this cookbook.

INGREDIENTS
2 pounds ground beef
1 stick (½ cup) butter
2 cups chopped onions
salt to taste
1½ quart water
1 tablespoon sugar
1½ teaspoons ground cloves
½ teaspoon cayenne pepper
1 tablespoon chili powder
1 tablespoon dry mustard
1 tablespoon paprika
1 tablespoon cinnamon
2 teaspoons turmeric
1½ teaspoons ground cumin
2-5 tablespoons cornstarch
½ cup cold water

Break up the ground beef well and cook over medium high heat. It should be browned with the onion and butter until very finely crumbled. Add the remaining ingredients except for the cornstarch. Simmer for 1 hour then thicken with the cornstarch mixed in cold water (in a jar, combine the water and cornstarch and shake until mixed well). This recipe is best if allowed to stand and is then reheated. It can be used as a chili sauce for both hot dogs and hamburgers. (For best results, the hot dogs should be covered in minced sweet onions and the sauce.) Refrigerate any leftover sauce.

Yield: 2 quarts

HOLIDAY CHEER EGGNOG
by Maggie Sefton

For many years, our family held an open house gathering in our home every December during the Christmas holiday season. Hot mulled wine and rich eggnog were always favorites. Here are two of those recipes. I included the Wassail Bowl (Hot Mulled Wine) recipe in the sixth **Kelly Flynn Knitting Mystery,** *Fleece Navidad,* and let Burt take ownership. This is the first time I've shared the eggnog recipe.

INGREDIENTS
¾ cup granulated sugar, divided
10 egg yolks, beaten
4 cups whole milk, scalded
½ teaspoon salt
10 egg whites
1 cup heavy cream, whipped
¾ cup light rum (or brandy)
Grated nutmeg

Blend ½ cup of the sugar and the egg yolks in the top part of a double boiler; stir in the milk slowly. Cook until the mixture coats a spoon, stirring constantly. Remove from the heat. Chill well. Add the salt to the egg whites and beat until stiff. Gradually beat in the remaining sugar. Fold the egg whites and whipped cream separately into the chilled custard mixture. Add rum (or brandy) and fold in gently. Chill for several hours. Pour into a punch bowl and sprinkle with nutmeg.

Yield: 16-20 servings

BURT'S WASSAIL

by Maggie Sefton

Enjoy—-and make sure you have a "designated driver" for the evening.

INGREDIENTS
6 cups of Burgundy or Claret
1 cup dry sherry
peels from two oranges and two lemons
1 6-inch stick cinnamon (broken into one-inch pieces)
2 whole nutmegs, crushed
10 whole cloves
2 tablespoons granulated sugar

Mix all ingredients in a saucepan or pot and simmer gently over low heat for 5 to 10 minutes—do not boil. Strain to remove the fruit peel and spices. Serve hot in a punchbowl or serving bowl with a ladle.

Yield: 12-14 servings

JILLIAN'S SWEET TEA

by Leann Sweeney

In every **Cats in Trouble Mystery,** quilter and cat lover Jillian Hart, her best friend Deputy Candace Carson, and her stepdaughter, Kara Hart, cannot get enough of this sweet tea. It's the much-needed Southern staple they all turn to when it's time to talk over a mystery, relax and chat, or just relieve stress. Some folks may turn to a stiff drink, but Jillian knows there always has to be a pitcher of tea in the fridge—winter or summer. Lemon is optional, ice is not.

INGREDIENTS FOR CANE SYRUP:
5-6 cups granulated sugar
3 cups cold water.

In a saucepan, combine the sugar and the cold water. Heat the liquid on medium-high until the sugar is dissolved and the liquid is clear (about 5 to 10 minutes). Cool and pour into a stoppered bottle. Use for sweetening the tea.

Yield: 1 quart

FOR THE TEA:
4-6 standard tea bags (the more you use the stronger the tea)
OR 1 ounce good quality loose tea (black tea—not green or white)
1 quart just-boiled water
1 quart room temperature water

Place the tea leaves or tea bags in the bottom of a metal or glass container (do not use a plastic container). Bring the water just to the boiling point where it's bubbling fully, but don't sustain the water at a rolling boil (over-boiling makes the tea taste flat). Pour the hot water over the bags and allow to steep for 6 to 7 minutes. Pour into a 2-quart pitcher, and add the room temperature water. Adding cold water, leads to cloudy tea. Allow to cool, or refrigerate. (Never dilute the tea with ice.)

To serve: fill a tall glass with ice. Pour the tea over it, and sweeten to taste. Give each guest a long spoon along with the bottle of sugar syrup for sweetening, as granulated sugar never quite all dissolves. Jillian pours about ½ cup of cane syrup into 2 quarts of tea when she's making this for herself and her regular tea drinking friends.

Yield: 2 quarts

HOT SPICED CIDER

by Kate Collins

This is a great recipe to fix in the winter for company, or (without the rum) for family coming home from sledding or skating.

INGREDIENTS
2 quarts apple cider
½ cup orange juice
¼ cup lemon juice
2 tablespoons sugar
6 whole cloves
6 whole or ½ teaspoon ground allspice
3 cinnamon sticks
1 teaspoon nutmeg
2 oranges, sliced
1 cup rum, optional

Tie the spices in cloth bag. Add to the liquids in a saucepan and boil for 3 minutes. Cool the cider mixture and remove the bag. Heat the spiced cider to the boiling point. Serve hot.

Yield: 8-9 servings

BELLE'S CHRISTMAS MOCHA GIFT MIX
by Leann Sweeney

Belle's Beans is the coffee shop where everyone in Mercy, South Carolina (home of the **Cats in Trouble Mysteries**) gathers to gossip and enjoy good coffee. Every Christmas, Belle makes up this mixture of coffee and chocolate and gives it in little jars to her favorite customers. This is the only time she ever uses instant coffee!

INGREDIENTS
1 cup dry non-dairy creamer
1 cup instant cocoa mix
⅔ cup instant coffee (you can even use a flavored one like French vanilla)
¼ or ½ cup granulated sugar (less if you are using a flavored instant coffee as they are already sweetened)
½ teaspoon cinnamon
¼ teaspoon nutmeg

Combine all the ingredients. For gifts, spoon into decorative glass jars or use a Christmas mug and seal with colored plastic wrap and a ribbon. On the tag, include these instructions: Mix 3-4 heaping teaspoons with 6 ounces of boiling water.

Yield: 5-6 servings

HOT BUTTERED RUM

by Deb Baker (aka Hannah Reed)

The holiday season wouldn't be the same without a big batch of hot buttered rum batter to serve to guests. ***The Queen Bee Mystery's*** Story Fischer makes it ahead of time and stores it in the fridge until the parties begin. Stu, down at Stu's Bar and Grill, has been after her for the recipe, but it's her little secret. And now it's yours, too.

INGREDIENTS
1 pound butter
2 pounds brown sugar
1½ teaspoon nutmeg
1½ teaspoon cinnamon
1 teaspoon vanilla
rum
hot water

Combine all the ingredients (it will make a paste which is called the "batter"). Mix 2½ tablespoons of the batter, 2 shots of your favorite rum, and fill a mug with 8 ounces of hot water. Stir until thoroughly mixed.

Yield: 2 pounds

Dear Friends,

Thank you for spending time with our characters and for trying out our recipes. We hope you've discovered a bevy of new and delicious dishes and perhaps, if we're fortunate, your curiosity about a certain character or two has been piqued.

To learn more about The Cozy Chicks and our works, please refer to the list of author names and website addresses following this note. Happy reading!

The Cozy Chicks

(CozyChicksBlog.com)

ABOUT THE AUTHORS

Ellery Adams grew up on a beach near the Long Island Sound. Having spent her adult life in a series of land-locked towns, she cherishes her memories of open water, violent storms, and the smell of the sea. Ms. Adams has held many jobs including caterer, retail clerk, car salesperson, teacher, tutor, and tech writer, all the while penning poems, children's books, and novels. She now writes full-time from her home in Virginia.

Visit her website: www.ElleryAdamsMysteries.com

The Books By The Bay Mysteries
A Killer Plot
A Deadly Cliche
The Last Word
Written In Stone
Poisoned Prose

The Charmed Pie Mysteries
Pies and Prejudice
Peach Pies and Alibis
Pecan Pies and Homicide

JB Stanley
The Collectibles Mysteries
A Killer Collection
A Deadly Appraisal
A Deadly Dealer

The Supper Club Mysteries
Carbs & Cadavers
Fit to Die
The Battered Body

Stiffs And Swine
Chili Con Corpses
Black Beans & Vice

Deb Baker writes the humorous award-winning *Gertie Johnson* mystery series set in the Michigan Upper Peninsula. She has also penned a doll collecting mystery series. As **Hannah Reed**, she writes about a Wisconsin beekeeper, who gets herself into some pretty sticky situations. When not struggling with her split personality, Deb gardens, cooks, reads, and kills people in her stories.

Visit Deb's website: www.deb-baker.blogspot.com
Hannah's website: www.QueenBeeMystery.com

Deb Baker
The Gertie Johnson Backwoods Mysteries
Murder Passes the Buck
Murder Grins and Bears It
Murder Talks Turkey
Murder Bites the Bullet
Murder Trims the Tree
Cooking Can Be Murder

The Dolls To Die For Mysteries
Dolled Up For Murder
Goodbye Dolly
Dolly Departed
Guise and Dolls

Hannah Reed
The Queen Bee Mysteries
Buzz Off
Mind Your Own Beeswax
Plan Bee
Beeline To Trouble
Beewitched

Scottish Highlands Mystery
Off Kilter

Lorraine Bartlett must be absolutely crazy. Why else would she write three different mystery series under three different names? They are: the *New York Times* bestselling Victoria Square Mysteries; the Jeff Resnick Mysteries as L.L. Bartlett; and the *New York Times* best-selling, Agatha-nominated Booktown Mysteries under the name Lorna Barrett. She lives in Rochester, NY with her husband and three cats, writing the days away.

Visit Lorraine's website: www.LorraineBartlett.com
L.L.'s website: www.LLBartlett.com
Lorna's website: www.LornaBarrett.com

The Victoria Square Mysteries
A Crafty Killing
The Walled Flower
One Hot Murder
Recipes To Die For: A Victoria Square Cookbook

L.L. Bartlett
The Jeff Resnick Mysteries
Murder On The Mind
Dead In Red
Room At The Inn
Cheated By Death
Bound By Suggestion
Dark Waters
Evolution: Jeff Resnick's Backstory

Lorna Barrett
The Booktown Mysteries
Murder Is Binding
Bookmarked For Death
Bookplate Special
Chapter & Hearse
Sentenced To Death
Murder On The Half Shelf
Not The Killing Type
Book Clubbed

Kate Collins is the author of the *New York Times* best-selling *Flower Shop Mystery* series. Her books have made the Barnes & Noble bestseller lists, the Independent Booksellers bestsellers lists, as well as lists in Australia and England. All of Kate's mysteries are available in print, digital, and large-print editions, both in the U.S. and in the UK. Kate's historical romances are also available in digital format from any e-book retailer. For more information on the *Flower Shop Mysteries*, visit Kate's website: KateCollinsBooks.com

The Flower Shop Mysteries
Mum's The Word
Slay It With Flowers
Dearly Depotted
Snipped In The Bud
Acts of Violets
A Rose From The Dead
Shoots to Kill
Evil in Carnations
Sleeping with Anemone
Dirty Rotten Tendrils
Night Of The Living Dandelion
To Catch A Leaf
Nighthad On Elm Street
Seed No Evil
Throw In The Trowel

Historical Romances
Promised To A Stranger
His Forbidden Touch
Courting Claire
Beloved Protector

Mary Kennedy is a former television news writer and the author of over 40 novels, including *The Talk Radio Mysteries* and the *Dream Club Mysteries.* She's a clinical psychologist in private practice and lives on the east coast with her husband and eight eccentric cats. Both husband and cats have resisted all her attempts to psychoanalyze them, but she remains optimistic.

Visit her website: www.MaryKennedy.net

The Dream Club Mysteries
Nightmares Can Be Murder
A Recipe For Murder
A Ghostly Murder

Talk Radio Mysteries
Dead Air
Reel Murder
Stay Tuned For Murder

Young Adult Novels
Movie Star
Heartbreakers
Golden Girl
Summer Nights

That shadowy figure known as **Victoria Abbott** is a collaboration between the always very funny and creative artist, photographer and short story author, Victoria Maffini and her mother, **Mary Jane Maffini**, award-winning author of three other mystery series and two dozen short stories. Originally from Nova Scotia, they now live near each other outside Ottawa, Ontario. You can catch their news and sign up for their newsletter at Mary Jane's website: www.MaryJaneMaffini.com
or the
Victoria Abbott website: www.Victoria-Abbott.com

The Charlotte Adams Mysteries
Organize Your Corpses
The Cluttered Corpse
Death Loves A Messy Desk
Closet Confidential
The Busy Woman's Guide To Murder

The Fiona Silk Mysteries
Lament for a Lounge Lizard
Too Hot To Handle

The Camilla MacPhee Mysteries
Speak Ill of the Dead
The Icing On The Corpse
Little Boy Blues
The Devil's In The Details
The Dead Don't Get Out Much
Law and Disorder

The Book Collector's Mysteries
The Christie Curse
The Sayers Swindle
The Wolfe Widow

Maggie Sefton is the *New York Times* Bestselling author of the **Kelly Flynn Knitting Mysteries**. Unraveled, ninth in the series, made the *New York Times* bestselling hardcover fiction List after its June 2011 release. Maggie's earlier published mystery, *Dying To Sell*, is now available as an e-book. Maggie's mystery series, set in Washington, DC begins with *Deadly Politics*. Maggie grew up in Northern Virginia and has been a CPA and a real estate agent in the Rocky Mountain West, but finds nothing can match creating worlds on paper. She lives in Colorado.

Visit her website: www.MaggieSefton.com

The Kelly Flynn Knitting Mysteries:
Needled To Death
A Deadly Yarn
A Killer Stitch
Dyer Consequences
Fleece Navidad
Dropped Dead Stitch
Skein Of The Crime
Unraveled
Cast On, Kill Off
Close Knit Killer
Yarn Over Murder

The Molly Malone Mysteries:
Deadly Politics
Poisoned Politics
Bloody Politics

Single Titles
Dying To Sell
Abilene Gambler
Scoundrels, Secrets, and Murder

New York Times bestselling mystery writer **Leann Sweeney**, originally from western New York, called Texas home for many years, and now lives in South Carolina. She writes two series, the *Yellow Rose Mysteries* set in and around Houston, and the *Cats in Trouble Mysteries* set in fictional Mercy, South Carolina. Leann lives with her husband, two cats (Wexford and Marlowe) and Rosie, the labradoodle. Some of her recipes came from her grandfather, a chef.

Visit her website: www.LeannSweeney.com

The Cats In Trouble Mysteries
The Cat, The Quilt and the Corpse
The Cat, The Professor and the Poison
The Cat, The Lady and the Liar
The Cat, The Wife and the Weapon
The Cat, The Mill and the Murder
The Cat, The Vagabond and the Victim

The Yellow Rose Mysteries
Pick Your Poison
A Wedding To Die For
Dead Giveaway
Shoot From The Lip
Pushing Up Bluebonnets

Grab a cup of coffee or tea
and come visit us at our blog!
CozyChicksBlog.com

182   THE COZY CHICKS KITCHEN

INDEX

63752072R00108

Made in the USA
Middletown, DE
09 February 2018